W9-CEW-395

Physical Characteristics of the Poodle

(from the American Kennel Club breed standard)

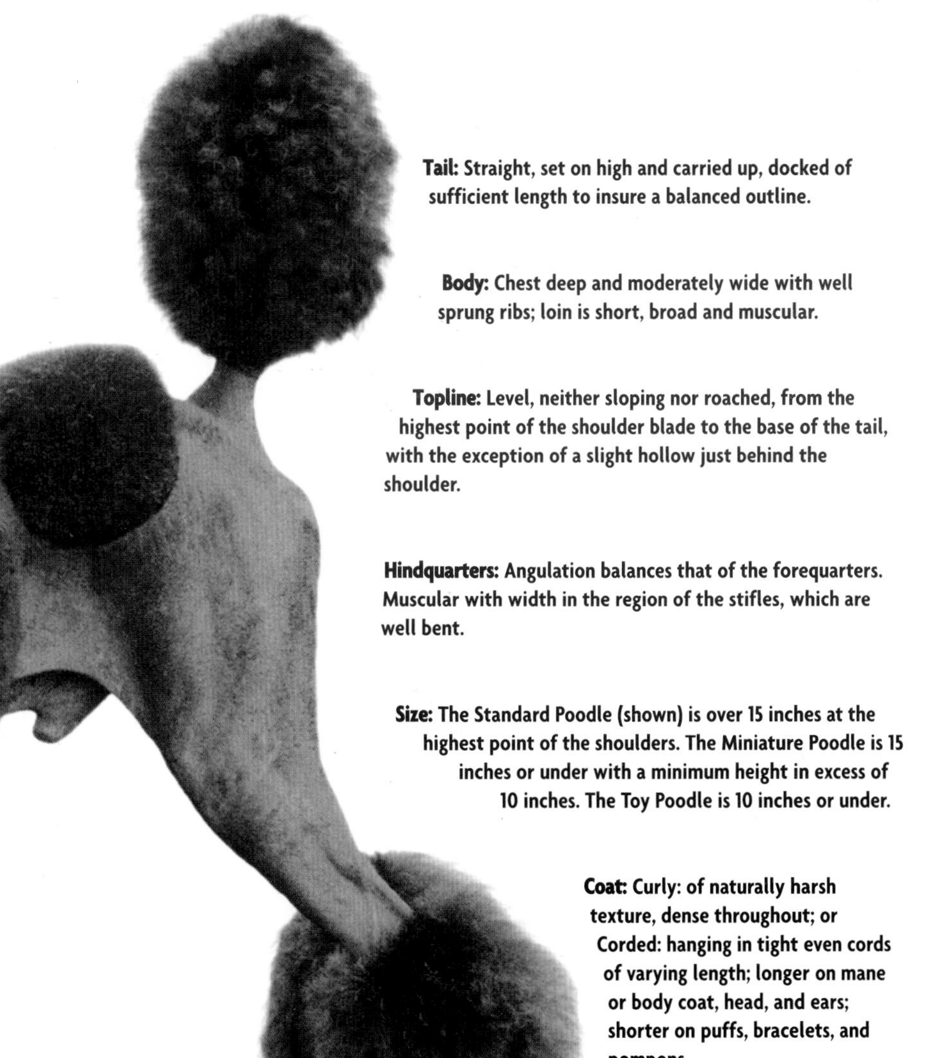

Tail: Straight, set on high and carried up, docked of sufficient length to insure a balanced outline.

Body: Chest deep and moderately wide with well sprung ribs; loin is short, broad and muscular.

Topline: Level, neither sloping nor roached, from the highest point of the shoulder blade to the base of the tail, with the exception of a slight hollow just behind the shoulder.

Hindquarters: Angulation balances that of the forequarters. Muscular with width in the region of the stifles, which are well bent.

Size: The Standard Poodle (shown) is over 15 inches at the highest point of the shoulders. The Miniature Poodle is 15 inches or under with a minimum height in excess of 10 inches. The Toy Poodle is 10 inches or under.

Coat: Curly: of naturally harsh texture, dense throughout; or Corded: hanging in tight even cords of varying length; longer on mane or body coat, head, and ears; shorter on puffs, bracelets, and pompons.

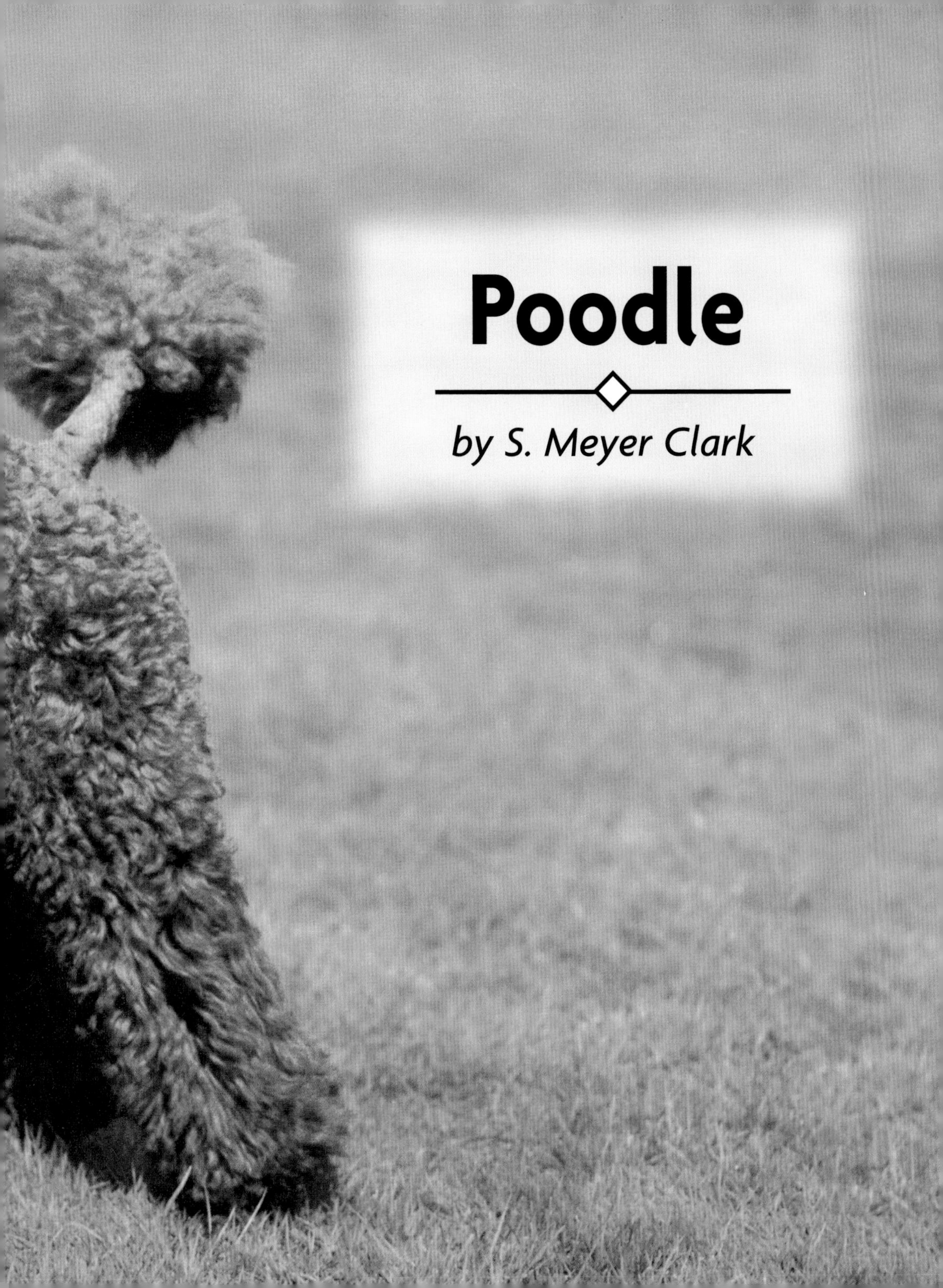

Poodle

by S. Meyer Clark

Contents

KENNEL CLUB BOOKS® **POODLE**

ISBN 13: 978-1-59378-243-6

Copyright © 2003, **2009** • Kennel Club Books® • A Division of BowTie, Inc.

40 Main Street, Freehold, NJ 07728 USA

Cover Design Patented: US 6,435,559 B2 • Printed in South Korea

All rights reserved. No part of this book may be reproduced in any form, by photostat, scanner, microfilm, xerography or any other means, or incorporated into any information retrieval system, electronic or mechanical, without the written permission of the copyright owner.

10 9 8 7

Photography by Carol Ann Johnson with additional photos by:

Norvia Behling, T. J. Calhoun, Carolina Biological Supply, Doskocil, Isabelle Français, James Hayden-Yoav, James R. Hayden, RBP, Bill Jonas, Dwight R. Kuhn, Dr. Dennis Kunkel, Antonio Philippe, Mikki Pet Products, Phototake, Jean Claude Revy, Dr. Andrew Spielman, Karen J. Taylor, Alice van Kempen and C. James Webb.

Illustrations by Renée Low.

The Publisher wishes to thank Anne Bondier, Barbara Cherry, Maryann K. Howarth, Carine Meyrueis, Lindy Miller, Stephen P. Regan, Gina Weiser and the rest of the owners of dogs featured in this book.

Germany is credited as being one of the breed's countries of origin, where Poodles were bred as water retrievers. Pictured here are Poodles in Germany at the turn of the 20th century, before entering a Berlin dog show.

HISTORY OF THE POODLE

Understanding the history of a breed allows us to better appreciate the various qualities of the breed and gives us a guideline by which we can judge the potential for companionship of an individual within that breed. While the Poodle is a purebred dog that is infinitely familiar to most people, let us examine the ancestry of the Poodle to learn more about this most intelligent and affectionate of all canines.

ORIGIN OF THE BREED

In the Middle Ages, from as far back as the 12th to the 15th century, Poodle-like dogs appeared in art and on carvings, coins and Roman tombs. This ancient breed has always displayed a unique style of coat, whether it was corded (hanging to the ground in long twists of hair) or curly and wiry (lending itself to hand-scissoring in a variety of patterned trims).

In modern times, three countries emerge as the original homes of the Poodle: Germany, Russia and France. All three countries presented their versions of the Poodle; each was designed for specific purposes. For example, the German Poodles were referred to as Pudel dogs.

Eng. Ch. Gondolette, bred by Miss H. C. Throwgood in 1924, was the daughter of two famous dogs of the time, Eng. Ch. Ambrette and Eng. Ch. Cadeau.

These dogs were heavy-boned and bred to retrieve fallen game, such as ducks, from the water—hence the name *Pudel*, which means "to splash in water."

The Russian Poodle was taller and more refined than its German cousin, thus lending itself to the role of companion dog. French Poodles were adored by the fashion world because their curly, woolly coats were ideal for elaborate grooming and styling. Their loving devotion to their owners also earned them high ratings.

When the Miniature Poodle eventually emerged in all three countries, it proved ideal as a circus dog. Owing to its intelligence and willingness to please, the Miniature Poodle was easy to train, appealing to audiences and easy to manage as the troupes moved from town to town.

Poodles were so popular in Europe that the famous Spanish painter Francisco de Goya rendered them in the 1700s. In fact, King Louis XVI of France commissioned Goya to create a portrait of a Poodle beloved by his wife, Marie Antoinette. Even before that, Albrecht Durer, a German artist, portrayed Poodles in his 15th-century paintings.

Many breed historians purport that, as far back as the first century, the Poodle was created by blending the white Maltese dog and the Spanish dog known as the Spaniel. Certainly both of these breeds could have contributed their friendly personalities to the Poodle's gene pool. Additionally, the Spaniel's love for water and its retrieving traits may be responsible for the Poodle's ability to retrieve fallen ducks from the water.

For centuries, the Poodle has been considered the height of fashion. Note that these Miniatures have bows on their topknots as well as around their wrists.

Regardless of their country of origin, Poodles have been and continue to be excellent retrievers. They love to carry things in their mouths and are easily trained to retrieve fallen game for hunters as well as toys and other objects for pet owners. In addition, their love of water and swimming makes them desirable as family companions in today's world. Boat owners and beach-goers alike find their Poodles eager to accompany them for sport and fun. Many Poodles even love to walk in the rain.

Until the 16th century, Poodles were large dogs known as Standards. They needed to be large, strong dogs, capable of retrieving fallen game, because they were primarily hunters' dogs. This work, however, created one serious problem. Since hunting back in the early times was for food rather than for sport, men in the Middle Ages needed a dog that would bring in game wherever it fell. However, when the game fell over the water, the heavily coated Poodle would often drown while attempting to retrieve the fallen bird. The Poodle's thick coat would soak up so much water that the dog could not stay afloat due to the weight of the water.

In Vienna, 1929, the Poodle, more especially the white Miniature variety, was considered among the most fashionable of companion dogs.

Hunters solved this problem by cutting off all unnecessary hair on the dog. Hair on the feet, face, tail and hindquarters was not needed, so it was trimmed away. Hair over the chest and around the lung and kidney areas was left to protect the

Eng. Ch. Barbet Chita was counted among Mrs. Crimmins' noted Miniature Poodles. Poodles bred under Mrs. Crimmins' Barbet prefix were some of the best of the time.

Here are typical examples of British dogs of the 1930s produced by Phidgity Kennels.

dog from the frigid waters. Thus was born the art of Poodle grooming, and this tradition remains mandatory for Poodles in the show ring today. The modern misconception that Poodle hairstyles make the dogs look overly feminine is rightly dispelled when one understands that cutting away the hair not needed for protection was necessary to make the dog more utilitarian.

During the 16th to 18th centuries, people began breeding smaller-sized Standard Poodles to create the Miniature Poodle. The Miniature became the ideal pet dog for the same reasons that he was used in circuses and stage shows: he was athletic, eager to please, attractive and affectionate.

No sooner had Miniature Poodles become popular with pet owners than breeders began developing an even smaller dog, the *Petit Barbet* or Toy Poodle. Originally they were called 'Sleeve Poodles' because they

Mrs. L. W. Crouch's Poodles, photographed in 1907 by T. Fall.

Poodles from the turn of the 20th century. Note their curly coats and smart topknots.

were so small that they could be carried around in the sleeves of ladies' gowns. The ladies of France, for example, loved the Toy Poodle because, when groomed properly, it was particularly clean and attractive.

Eng. Ch. Barbet Mala Sirius was a Miniature Poodle owned by Mrs. Crimmins and bred by Miss Kalender in 1930. Mala Sirius won her first honors at a UK Championship Show in 1931.

NEXT STOP: GREAT BRITAIN

Once all three sizes of Poodle were firmly established on the Continent, it was inevitable that they cross the channel to the British Isles. The English people received them with open arms, as did the dog-show world throughout England. In the mid-19th century, Sir Edwin Landseer memorialized the breed in some of his family portraits.

Miniature Poodle, painted by the famed dog artist Maud Earl.

Poodle popularity in Great Britain simply confirmed what Europeans had known for centuries: Poodles of every size are ideal companions, whether for work as hunters or as family pets. In addition, older people who lived alone found that bringing an easy-to-care-for Toy Poodle into their homes added a new quality to their lives.

Poodle history suggests that the English Water Dog was created by crossing the Poodle with some other breeds. We know for certain that Toy Poodles were used in the development of the Truffle Dog. Truffles, the famous delicacy, are located and unearthed by the small Poodles. Their light weight and gentle steps, combined with their excellent scenting ability, make them perfect dogs for truffle hunting. Terriers were eventually added to the mix for their digging habits, thus creating the Truffle Dog.

Circa 1920, King Leo of Piperscroft was the first Poodle to compete in an obedience trial in Britain. He did remarkably well and thus earned further recognition for Mrs. Boyd's well-known kennels.

Standard Poodles in pet trim, the simplest and most convenient clip for a pet owner to maintain. Show dogs cannot be trimmed in this fashion.

Eng. Ch. Orchard Admiral, photographed in 1907 by T. Fall.

THE POODLE ARRIVES IN AMERICA

It was inevitable that, from England, Poodles would find their way to America. They did so in 1887. Prior to World War I, Poodle popularity reached a peak at American dog shows. Originally,

The Poodle was, at one time, one of the world's most popular dogs, especially with lady fanciers. Consequently, breeders vied with one another to develop the coat, which ranged from thick curls to long but orderly cords. This photo, dated 1899, shows a typical high-quality corded Poodle. The corded coat is much less common than the curly coat.

Standards and Miniatures in America were shown as a single breed, and Toys were shown as a separate breed prior to World War II.

The Poodle Club of America, founded in 1931 to govern the standard of perfection for all Poodles, offered classes with the same criteria for all three sizes. As a matter of fact, the first Miniature to earn an American championship title was the black English dog named Ch. Chieveley Chopstick.

Some of England's finest Poodles as well as several from the Continent were imported to America during the early 1900s. Their genetic heritage still carries on today, and we often see the names of well-known English dogs in the pedigrees of modern American Poodles.

By 1960, America had caught up with the British and European interest in the breed. Poodles became the most popular breed of dog in American Kennel Club registra-

Miss Jane Lane, who made a considerable positive impact on the Poodle fancy through her Nunsoe kennels, is shown with her favorites, Int. Ch. Nunsoe Duc de la Terrace and Ch. Nunsoe Lady Mary.

tion statistics. They have maintained the status of being among the ten most popular breeds ever since.

One reason for the Poodle's elite standing in dogdom is the breed's affinity for obedience competition. Aside from excelling in the conformation show ring, Poodles love attention, and performing in obedience to please their owners and others is a terrific way of getting attention.

In the 1930s, Helen Whitehouse Walker, owner of Carillon Kennels, wanted to introduce the sport of obedience into America. She was tired of hearing people say that Poodles, with their fancy hairdos, were

Right: Reserve Best in Show and winner of the Group at the Royal Show in Sydney, Australia was Standard Poodle Aust. Ch. Troymere Believe in Me. This is what a modern champion looks like.

The famed Poodle breeder, Miss Florence Brunker, though well-known for her excellent Poodles, was also famous for her extravagant hats. She prided herself in having hats larger than her dogs, or, alternatively, having dogs smaller than her hats.

This smartly trimmed black Standard will be taking a ribbon home for his equally smartly dressed handler.

vanity dogs. She vowed to prove the Poodle's intelligence and trainability to America.

In 1934, as England was enjoying the growing sport of obedience trialing, Mrs. Walker went to Great Britain to study the sport and the training methods for obedience. When she returned home to America, she shared what she had learned with others, including her dear friend, Blanche Sauders, who ultimately became a renowned obedience exhibitor and teacher.

By 1947, America was ready to recognize obedience competition. The American Kennel Club officially adopted the rules and regulations for the sport and established an obedience department within its ranks.

From the working Poodle-like dogs of Europe in the 12th century to the sophisticated Poodles of the 21st century, the breed maintains its ancestral traits that endear it to people around the world. Thus, centuries after the breed's development, there seems no reason to believe that Poodles will be any less popular in the future than they have been in the past.

Standard Poodle being gaited around the ring. The evaluation of a dog's movement determines how well-constructed the animal is.

CHARACTERISTICS OF THE POODLE

The Poodle, regardless of size or color, is a distinctive, squarely built, elegant dog with a coat that serves as the crowning touch to a royal entity. From the largest Standard to the tiniest Toy, Poodles have a unique way about them that transcends everything they do in life. How they carry themselves when out for a walk, the easy sway of the hind legs as they chase a ball across a lawn, the alert inquisitive expression when they hear a familiar voice—these traits are all special to Poodles. And every owner quickly learns to recognize that Poodle uniqueness.

This lovely black male is kept in immaculate condition.

In addition to loving life in general, Poodles love people even more. They are particularly perceptive of our moods and emotions, and respond accordingly. They join in celebrations when we're happy and hover nearby in quiet concern when we're ill, worried or sad.

They are extremely intelligent and can learn an amazing repertoire of commands if taught with patience and kindness. Retrieving fallen ducks and carrying things in their mouths are but a sample of their rehearsed behaviors. Ever since early Poodle owners discovered the breed's propensity to learn, Poodles have been trained to perform many behaviors, from helping owners around the home to dancing in circus acts around the world.

Poodles love to please. They crave attention and have an uncanny sense of humor. If, for example, a Poodle does something that an owner finds amusing and

A Standard apricot with white Miniatures. The variety of sizes and striking colors offers many choices to prospective Poodle owners.

the person responds with laughter and praise, the dog will quickly pick up this response and repeat the behavior over and over. In short, Poodles are genetically "programmed" to work with humans and use their own emotional intuitiveness to create strong bonds with their owners.

The physical makeup of Poodles is such that they can perform many athletic feats with ease. Standing on their hind legs and "dancing," climbing to heights on ladders and ramps, jumping all types of barriers and sitting on their haunches to "beg" are just some of the Poodle's agile maneuvers. These and many more stunts are possible due to the breed's exceptional sense of balance and dexterity.

Combine intelligence, emotional intuitiveness, love of companionship, physical ability and beauty in one breed of dog and you have the remarkable, personable Poodle. This breed is of such great versatility, it's no wonder that Poodles are considered to be the most intelligent of all breeds.

DIFFERENT SIZES, DIFFERENT PERSONALITIES

Poodles come in a wide range of sizes. Toy Poodles stand 10 inches or less at the shoulder. Miniatures stand 15 inches or under, but

A lovely black champion Miniature Poodle. The breed's show coat presentation is exquisite.

must be taller than 10 inches at the shoulder. Standards must stand over 15 inches at the shoulder. In some European circles, there is a fourth size called Moyen, which means "middle" or in between the Miniature and the Standard. Moyens measure at least 15 inches but rarely reach the height of the average Standard. Certainly there is a size of Poodle for every lifestyle and taste.

Different-sized Poodles frequently exhibit different

Posing with his tortoise playmates, this Toy Poodle pup is photogenic and fun-spirited.

When dogs are a family affair, the Poodles never shy away from participation. Dyed purple to match the bride's bouquet, these two Poodles were the matrons of honor at the wedding of Meg Purnell's daughter, Rachel, and her dapper husband, Darren. The family runs the well-known Overhill Kennels in England.

The Standard Poodle is every inch a Poodle, with a good sense of humor and impressive protective instincts.

Regardless of size, Poodles share certain characteristics, from their people-friendly personality to their eye-opening intelligence.

behavioral traits. For example, the handsome Standard is every inch a Poodle with his bright expressive eyes, his devotion to owner and family, his love of learning and his sense of humor. In addition, he carries himself with great confidence and therefore excels as a guardian of home and family. He is serious enough and big enough to make the consequences of unwanted entry most undesirable. His deep bark and courageous demeanor send an instant message to any and all unwelcome guests that a forced entry would be most unwise.

I once owned a large chocolate Standard who was very protective of home and family. On two separate occasions, he leaped through a glass window to chase away suspected prowlers on my property. Fortunately for the individuals, I was at home on both occasions and stopped the dog from further action against the men. However, they didn't linger about to find out how serious and strong the dog was.

Standard Poodles are large enough to tolerate the pulling and pushing of toddlers who cling to their soft coat for support when they're learning to walk. The dogs are also gentle enough, when raised with children, to be sympathetic to children older than toddlers who run and squeal as they play.

The Miniature Poodle is an active, agile, alert dog of medium build whose appearance suggests a curious interest in everything in his environment. Miniature Poodles are people-pleasers from the word "go." They are also great

Miniature Poodles are remarkable dogs, being friendly, courageous, active, easily trained and fun to be with.

alarm dogs, warning of the approach of strangers. They are small enough to travel well, adapt to any type of dwelling from small apartment to large estate and friendly enough to join any group at a social gathering. Children and adults alike respond to their quick wit and pleasant attitude toward all who know them.

The Miniature also serves as an alternative size for people who have spent their lives loving Standard Poodles but find that they no longer can maintain such a large dog. Their love of Poodles in general is life-long, so changing to Miniature Poodle ownership is a natural step.

Finally, we come to the Toy Poodle, also a great alarm dog, if slightly higher pitched. The Toy looks the part of a lovely, delicate toy with an intense awareness of his owners and others in his world. These diminutive little treasures fill very special needs for special people. Because they're so small, they can be carried easily wherever their owners want to take them. Hotels usually accept them with no trouble; trains, ships and airplanes allow them to travel right along with the passengers rather than in cargo areas. In addition, they can be trained to eliminate indoors, thus diminishing the need to walk them outdoors daily. People who live in severe climates and those

Lovely lady...lovely Poodle. Poodles have been favorites of ladies for generations. While ladies usually favored Toy Poodles, Miniature Poodles also became popular because they are more adaptable and sporting than the Toys.

Poodles welcome children as playmates, provided the children are well behaved and understand that Poodles deserve considerate, special treatment.

who live in big cities where walking alone outdoors at night can be unsafe can own a Toy Poodle without worry. As for exercise, games and activities indoors can supply Toy Poodles with adequate exercise and stimulation. They also make ideal companions for elderly people with limited ambulatory ability.

Finally, tiny Toy Poodles make ideal partners for people who enjoy active lifestyles yet want to include their dogs in everything they do. A client of mine, for example, has a tiny apricot Poodle that rides around in a canvas bag that she carries over her shoulder. If you were to meet her in the market, you'd never know that hidden in that bag is her best friend, Toby. Apparently, Toby enjoys the gentle swaying of the bag as his owner walks along, so he snuggles into his soft blanket and naps throughout the entire shopping trip.

OWNER SUITABILITY

First and foremost, the new Poodle owner must consider the grooming requirements of Poodles, regardless of size. This is a life-long need and one that cannot be ignored. Some owners choose to groom their Poodles themselves and purchase the necessary tools to keep their dogs neat and tidy at all times.

Poodles are more fun to collect than postage stamps or coins! What could make your household more exciting than oodles of Poodles?

Others use professional groomers to keep their dogs looking their best. Either way, the Poodle must be fully groomed about every six to eight weeks, along with daily brushing and weekly bathing. The time and costs that this will entail must be considered before purchasing the dog.

Some Poodle owners elect to combine the two grooming methods. They have their dogs professionally groomed every eight weeks and, in between grooming, they do a lot to maintain that elegant appearance. They learn to trim toenails, clean ears, brush properly and bathe regularly. By taking care of the routine grooming between professional appointments, the owner assures that the coat will not become knotted or matted (the groomer will charge dearly to remove mats from the coat).

An ideal Poodle owner should be a person who enjoys the intelligence and versatility of the breed. Poodles do not make good "couch potatoes." Regardless of size, they are active dogs that need to keep busy and be challenged and stimulated on a daily basis.

They also do not fare well with owners who don't spend time with them. The Poodle who has to stay home alone for hours on end and then remains alone even after the owner has finished his work day will not be a happy dog. Poodles have large egos and

Although larger than the ultra-portable Toy, the Miniature Poodle is willing and able to accompany his owner most anywhere.

need to be active parts of their owners' lives, whether that life includes hiking in the park or strolling along the seashore, or anything in between. Accompanying their owners when visiting friends is another favorite pastime of Poodles, and they make great house guests!

One of the Poodle's favorite activities can be attending obedience classes or entering obedience trials. In every country where obedience trials are conducted, Poodles rank high on the lists of winners because of their intelligence and willingness to please.

Finally, the Poodle owner should be a person who loves life, enjoys laughter and looks forward to greeting each new day as much as his Poodle does.

Poodle owners should be people who appreciate the finer qualities of their dogs. A sense of humor and an exuberant love of life are among the traits that owner and Poodle should share.

PHYSICAL CHARACTERISTICS

A Poodle should be as tall from the ground to the top of his withers (shoulders) as he is long from the tip of his chest to his rump. The topline (the line of the backbone from shoulder to hip) should be parallel to the ground. His tail should be carried gaily and sport a full pompon at the tip. Poodle feet are shaved clean, as is the face (with the exception of pet males, who may wear mustaches). Poodle ears are long, full and always free of mats and foreign matter. The top of the Poodle skull is covered by a pompon known as a topknot. This topknot adds height to the dog and a distinctive frame around the bright eyes and long muzzle.

Poodle puppies are affectionate and outgoing charmers—one cuddle and you'll be hooked!

COAT AND GROOMING

The Poodle's coat consists of two types of hair. The outer coat should be thick, wiry and curly. The undercoat must be soft and woolly to provide warmth. Puppies, however, are exceptions. Poodle puppy coats are soft and fine with little or no curl, but often with a slight wave. As the dog matures into adulthood, the coat develops a thick, curly quality. The best way to judge a puppy's potential adult coat is to look at the parents. If they carry good coats, their puppies will likely possess them too.

Ever since the first hunters trimmed their retrieving dogs to prevent drowning, the Poodle hairstyle has been a favorite topic of conversation among dog people. Initially, Poodles sported either a Continental clip or an

English Saddle clip. Now, hundreds of years later, these are still popular; they are required clips for show dogs.

Puppies under one year of age are shown in a simple trim known as a Puppy clip. Only the face, throat, feet and base of tail are clipped. The tail displays the characteristic pompom at its end. The body coat is lightly trimmed to give it a neat unbroken line for a pleasant appearance.

The Continental clip has full hair around the chest and rib cage, with shaved hindquarters and legs. Large pompons are sculpted over each hip above the area of the kidneys (optional) and around the ankles for protection from the cold.

The English Saddle clip permits a short mantle of hair over the hindquarters and full coat from the waist to the topknot and ears. The ankle and knee joints are also protected with pompons.

All Poodles are given a topknot of hair over the skull that is brushed out and groomed to stand erect in a rounded pompon. Adult dogs must be

A Toy Poodle, sporting the Lion clip, the clip in which dogs are shown in the UK.

Fabuleux the Man in Black sets an excellent example of a well-bred, well-groomed Miniature Poodle.

Poodles have the most abundant and adaptable coats in the dog world—perhaps in the whole animal world. They do not shed as do most other dogs, but their coats require regular brushing and trimming.

A black male, from the Netherlands, perfectly groomed and perfectly poised. Poodles have always remained popular in Europe.

shown in either the English Saddle or Continental clip; the only exception being competitors in Stud Dog and Brood Bitch classes, for which a Sporting clip is permitted. The English Saddle and Continental are the clips of choice for the conformation ring around the world, except in the UK, where the Lion clip is preferred.

In the obedience ring, Poodles may be groomed in whatever style their owners desire, as their behavior and willingness to work with their owners are being judged, not their conformation.

Pet Poodles and those not being shown in breed conformation classes at dog shows are usually groomed in styles designed for ease of maintenance. Often the body hair is clipped short, with the legs trimmed a bit longer. Some male Poodles sport tiny mustaches around the muzzles. The pet style is usually determined by the owner's willingness and capability to maintain the coat in a well-groomed fashion. In addition, Poodles that spend a lot of time outdoors are usually kept shorter because it's easier to keep the coat clean when the hair isn't too long.

While on the subject of coat, we must mention the fact that Poodles don't shed or have an odor. Like that of humans, the hair keeps growing, which means that Poodles must be groomed on a frequent and regular basis all their lives. Poodles are high-maintenance dogs, and grooming can be costly and time-

Although there are dozens of clips used for Poodles worldwide, the Continental and English Saddle (shown here) remain the most popular for Poodle fanciers.

Top, left: A black Standard Poodle youngster in show stance. This clip is often called a Puppy clip.

Top, right: An elegantly groomed white Standard Poodle in Continental clip with hip pompons.

A Miniature Poodle in a typical English Saddle clip.

consuming. On the other hand, because Poodles do not shed, they are among only a few breeds whose hair will never be found on furniture and clothing, a real advantage. Many people who are allergic to dogs find that they can live without adverse reactions to Poodles because of this phenomenon.

When the topknot is full, it must be brushed out carefully to stand erect in a rounded pompon.

Color

Poodle colors are mind-boggling! For the purists, there are three choices: black, white and dark brown. For the more adventuresome, there are literally dozens of other shades, starting with cream to café-au-lait to pale apricot all the way to a deep, rich apricot that sparkles in the sunshine. From there, you can see deeper shades that reach eventually into rich chocolate brown. From coal black, you can descend to a deep gunmetal gray to various shades of plain gray and on toward silver-gray.

Poodle puppies are often born darker in color than they will be as adults. Gray Poodles, for example, are born black, while dark chocolate puppies usually lighten to a soft milk-chocolate shade.

I have owned Poodles in black, gunmetal gray, light and medium gray, chocolate brown, deep apricot and even light butterscotch. As far as I'm concerned, choosing just the right dog to live with does not depend

Despite the large number of colors and shades that Poodles can exhibit, the most commonly seen Poodle color is probably white. Whatever the color, it must be solid in show dogs; parti-colored dogs are disqualified.

Identifying the color of a Poodle can be perplexing. Some might call this a chocolate while others would say dark apricot.

on its color. There are far more important features to consider than the color.

One last note on color, however. It's important to point out here that café-au-lait and brown Poodles have dark amber eyes rather than the traditional black eyes. Also, their lips, eye rims and noses should be liver-colored instead of black. Apricots may have liver pigmentation and dark amber eyes, but black is preferred. In selecting a Poodle for

From gunmetal to silver, there is a magnificent range of gray shades seen in the Poodle.

A well-appreciated color is the apricot with a black nose.

showing, clear colors are preferred; solid colors are required.

HEALTH CONCERNS

Well-bred Poodles are hardy, long-lived dogs who enjoy good health all their days. However, Poodles can be subject to certain health conditions, and the wise Poodle puppy buyer should be aware of these problems and avoid them whenever possible.

As with humans, Poodles have many health concerns that are hereditary in nature. Many of these can be avoided by careful investigation on the new owner's part by asking the breeder about the health background of the puppy's parents. For example, have the parents been tested for such conditions as cataracts that can cause blindness? Does either of the parents have epilepsy and, if so, how is it controlled? Has either parent experienced orthopedic problems and, if so, how serious were they?

Here we take a closer look at some health conditions that have been found in Poodles as well as many other breeds of dog. Please note that not all Poodles experience these conditions. However, it behooves the puppy buyer to be well informed regarding potential health concerns of the breed under consideration. Also note that responsible breeders do not breed from any dog that is known to have or carry any hereditary problems.

Most Poodles are as "healthy as a horse," and some even get along well with an equine pal.

EYE PROBLEMS

A cataract is a cloudiness or film over the lens of the eye, categorized by age of onset, location on the eye and stage of the cloudiness. This condition is hereditary, and parents should be tested before breeding takes place to prevent this condition from being passed on.

Glaucoma, a leading cause of blindness, is caused by an increase in fluid pressure within the eye. It can be hereditary, and parents should be tested prior to breeding. Miniature Poodles are prone to narrow-angle glaucoma,

These two darlings are the picture of health. Poodles usually are healthy dogs and live long lives if properly cared for.

which produces pain and redness in the eyes. The treatment is medical and/or surgical.

Progressive retinal atrophy, or PRA, refers to inherited disorders affecting the retina of the eye. Visual impairment is slow but progressive. Night blindness can be the first signal of trouble, and there is no known way to stop onset.

Other conditions of the eye that have been observed in the Poodle include corneal dystrophy, congenital night blindness, entropion and tear duct anomalies.

Skin Problems

Atopic dermatitis refers to an unusual or atypical condition of the derma or skin. It can be difficult to diagnose.

Sebaceous adenitis is inflammatory damage to hair follicles and sebaceous glands. It is most often seen in Standard Poodles but also seen in Toys and Miniatures. It is a hereditary condition. There is no known cure, but treatment to control it includes frequent bathing to reduce surface scale and to increase moisture to the skin.

Color dilution alopecia is an anomaly that usually occurs in dogs bred for unusual coat colors, such as those described as "blue," which is a diluted form of black. The condition, when it occurs, is not curable. Moisturizers and frequent shampooing can lessen the incidence of dry, scaly skin.

Seborrhea is an abnormal and excessive discharge from the sebaceous glands in the skin; it must be treated medically.

Orthopedic Problems

Cruciate ligament injury is a condition in which diagonally crossed ligaments in the rear leg are injured and must be corrected surgically. This condition is painful to the dog.

Elbow dysplasia, also known as osteochondrosis, is often found in young growing dogs. It is genetic. Dogs allowed to exercise in excess are often at risk for this condition. The Orthopedic Foundation for Animals (OFA) has implemented a screening procedure in which dogs' elbows are x-rayed and the x-rays are examined and evaluated. Abnormal elbows are graded based on the severity of the dysplasia, while normal elbows of dogs 24 months old and older receive OFA certification. This scheme is designed to help identify dysplastic dogs and to help breeders eliminate affected dogs from their breeding programs.

Hip dysplasia is similar to elbow dysplasia; it is a genetically acquired problem of the hips in which the head of the femur does not fit correctly into the hip joint. The OFA also has a screening program for hips, in which hip x-rays of dogs at least 24 months old are evaluated and graded in one of seven categories: Excellent, Good, Fair, Borderline, Mild, Moderate and Severe. Only hips graded Fair or better are given OFA numbers. Again, this screening process identifies dysplastic dogs to help breeders to select healthy breeding stock free of genetic defects.

Legg-Calve-Perthes disease is a disorder of the hip joint, often seen in young small-breed dogs, which causes lameness and pain in one leg. Surgical removal of the femoral head is the usual treatment.

Kneecap dislocation or medial patellar luxation occurs when the kneecap slips out of place and rests on the inside of the knee. This condition is mostly seen in small dogs. Therapy may help, but surgery is more frequently used to relieve the problem. It is most probably genetic in origin.

Other Problems

Following are brief descriptions of some conditions seen in many breeds and that can occur in the Poodle.

Bloat or stomach torsion is a condition in which the stomach twists over and fills with air, releasing toxins into the bloodstream. This requires immediate medical help. It can be fatal if not treated early enough. This condition is usually a concern for deep-chested breeds and may affect the Standard Poodle; your vet can advise you of precautionary measures against bloat.

Cushing's syndrome is a pituitary disorder in which the body produces too much cortisone. It is medically treatable.

Hypothyroidism is a hormone problem usually seen in older dogs. It can be treated by a veterinarian.

Patent ductus heart disease is a congenital heart defect that is genetic. Surgery is required for correction.

Epilepsy is a disorder characterized by a seizure in the brain that can be controlled with medication.

Von Willebrand's disease is genetic in nature. It is a bleeding disorder in which a low clotting factor can prove fatal. Dogs should be tested for clotting factor prior to surgery.

BREED STANDARD FOR THE POODLE

A breed standard is the blueprint of the dog, a written description of what breeders and judges are looking for in a perfect Poodle, both physically and temperamentally. While there has never been a "perfect" Poodle, nor a flawless example of any breed, breeders use the standard as a set of goals for which to strive. Judges use the standard to evaluate how well the breeders are doing in reaching that goal.

Poodles are compared to a breed standard in the show ring. The dog that most closely "conforms" to the standard is regarded as the best.

The following description is excerpted from the standard of the American Kennel Club (AKC). Those interested in showing should obtain the complete standard to acquaint themselves with all details, faults and disqualifications.

THE AKC STANDARD FOR THE POODLE

The standard for the Poodle (Toy variety) is the same as for the Standard and Minature varieties except as regards height.

General Appearance, Carriage and Condition

That of a very active, intelligent and elegant-appearing dog, squarely built, well proportioned, moving soundly and carrying himself proudly.

Size, Proportion, Substance

Size: The Standard Poodle is over 15 inches at the highest point of the shoulders. The Miniature Poodle is 15 inches or under at the highest point of the shoulders, with a minimum height in excess of 10 inches. The Toy Poodle is 10 inches or under at the highest point of the shoulders.

Proportion: To insure the desirable squarely built appearance, the length of body measured from the breastbone to the point of the rump approximates the height from the highest point of the shoulders to the ground.

Substance: Bone and muscle of both forelegs and hindlegs are in proportion to size of dog.

Head and Expression

(a) Eyes—very dark, oval in shape and set far enough apart and positioned to create an alert intelligent expression.

(b) Ears—hanging close to the head, set at or slightly below eye level. The ear leather is long, wide and thickly feathered.

(c) Skull—moderately rounded, with a slight but definite stop. Cheekbones and muscles flat.

The physical attributes of a Poodle are measured against the standard as are gait and temperament.

(d) Muzzle—long, straight and fine, with slight chiseling under the eyes. Strong without lippiness. The chin definite enough to preclude snipiness. Teeth— white, strong and with a scissors bite.

The correct Poodle head has a moderately rounded skull and a long, straight, fine muzzle.

Neck, Topline, Body

Neck well proportioned, strong and long enough to permit the head to be carried high and with dignity. The neck rises from strong, smoothly muscled shoulders. The topline is level, neither sloping nor roached, with the exception of a slight hollow just behind the shoulder.

Incorrect muzzle; too much chin.

Correct head in profile.

Body

(a) Chest deep and moderately wide with well sprung ribs.

(b) The loin is short, broad and muscular.

(c) Tail straight, set on high and carried up, docked of

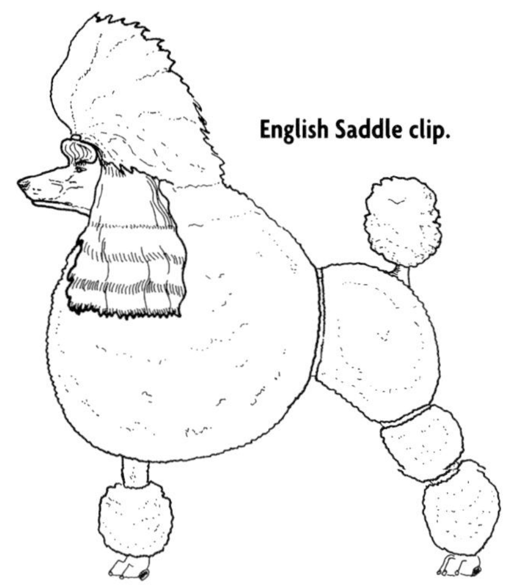

English Saddle clip.

sufficient length to insure a balanced outline.

Forequarters

Strong, smoothly muscled shoulders. The shoulder blade is well laid back. Forelegs straight and parallel when viewed from the front. Dewclaws may be removed.

Feet

The feet are rather small, oval in shape with toes well arched and cushioned on thick firm pads. The feet turn neither in nor out.

Hindquarters

The angulation of the hindquarters balances that of the forequarters. Hind legs straight and parallel when viewed from the rear.

Coat

(a) Quality—(1) Curly: of naturally harsh texture, dense

Standard Lion clip without hip pompon.

throughout. (2) Corded: hanging in tight even cords of varying length, longer on mane or body coat, head, and ears; shorter on puffs, bracelets, and pompons.

(b) Clip— A Poodle under 12 months may be shown in the Puppy clip. In all regular classes, Poodles 12 months or over must be shown in the English Saddle or Continental clip. In the Stud Dog and Brood Bitch classes and in a non-competitive Parade of Champions, Poodles may be shown in the Sporting clip. A Poodle shown in any other type of clip shall be disqualified.

(1) Puppy—A Poodle under a year old may be shown in the Puppy clip with the coat long. The face, throat, feet and base of the tail are shaved. There is a pompon on the end of the tail. (2) English Saddle—In the English Saddle clip the face, throat, feet, forelegs and base of the tail are shaved, leaving puffs on the forelegs and a pompon on the end of the tail. The hindquarters are covered with a

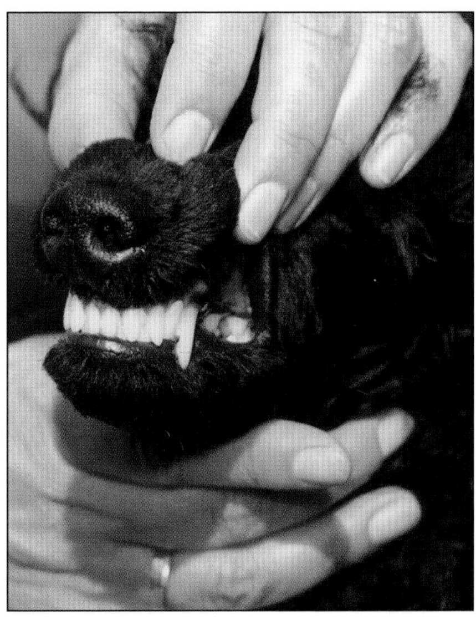

The Poodle has strong teeth in a scissors bite.

short blanket of hair except for a curved shaved area on each flank and two shaved bands on each hindleg. (3) Continental— In the Continental clip, the face,

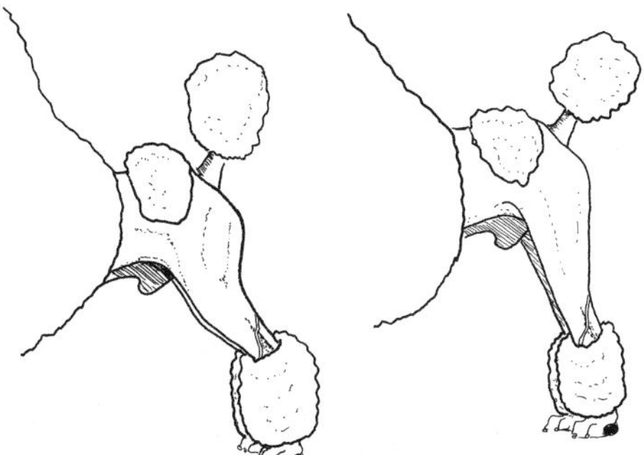

Correct angulation of rear. Incorrect rear; stifle straight.

Puppy clip.

Puppy clip showing the body outline.

The Lion clip is the clip of choice in the UK, where dogs are judged against the breed standard of The Kennel Club.

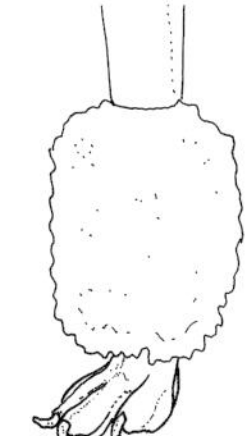

Incorrect foot.

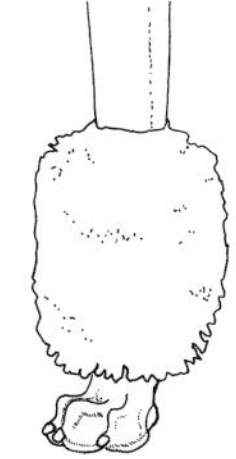

Correct foot.

throat, feet, and base of the tail are shaved. The hindquarters are shaved with pompons (optional) on the hips. The legs are shaved, leaving bracelets on the hindlegs and puffs on the forelegs. There is a pompon on the end of the tail. (4) Sporting—In the Sporting clip, a Poodle shall be shown with face, feet, throat and base of tail shaved, leaving a scissored cap on the top of the head and a pompon on the end of the tail. The rest of the body, and legs are clipped or scissored to follow the outline of the dog.

In all clips the hair of the topknot may be left free or held in place by elastic bands.

Color

The coat is an even and solid color at the skin. In blues, grays, silvers, browns, café-au-laits, apricots and creams, the coat may show varying shades of the same color. Brown and café-au-lait Poodles have liver-colored noses, eye-rims and lips, dark toenails and dark amber eyes. Black, blue, gray, silver, cream and white Poodles have black noses, eye-rims and lips, black or self colored toenails and very dark eyes. In the apricots, while the foregoing coloring is preferred, liver-colored noses, eye-rims and lips, and amber eyes are permitted but are not desirable.

Gait

A straightforward trot with light springy action and strong hindquarters drive. Head and tail carried up. Sound effortless movement is essential.

Temperament

Carrying himself proudly, very active, intelligent, the Poodle has about him an air of distinction and dignity peculiar to himself.

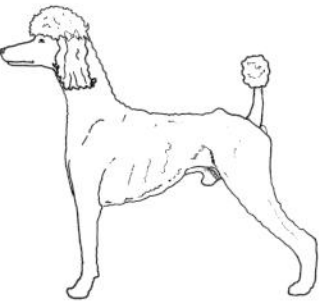

Underweight body.

Body at ideal weight.

Overweight body.

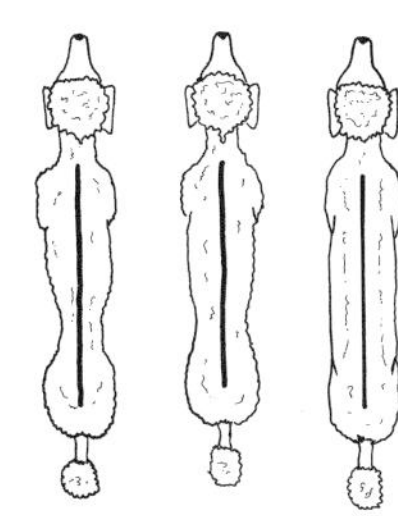

Left to right: underweight; ideal; overweight.

YOUR PUPPY

POODLE

WHERE TO BEGIN?

If you are convinced that the Poodle is the ideal dog for you, it's time learn about where to find a puppy and what to look for. Locating a litter of Poodles in any size should not present a problem for the new owner. You should inquire about breeders in your area who enjoy a good reputation in the breed. You are looking for an established breeder with outstanding dog ethics and a strong commitment to the breed. New owners should have as many questions as they have doubts. An established breeder is indeed the one to answer your many questions and make you comfortable with your choice of the Poodle. An established breeder will sell you a puppy at a fair price if, and only if, the breeder determines that you are a suitable, worthy owner of his/her dogs. An established breeder can be relied upon for advice, no matter what

A lifetime of knowledge comes from meeting the dam of your prospective Poodle puppy. Not only the physical attributes, coat quality and good health but also the temperament and personality are passed from generation to generation.

ARE YOU PREPARED?

Unfortunately, when a puppy is bought by someone who does not take into consideration the time and attention that dog ownership requires, it is the puppy who suffers when he is either abandoned or placed in a shelter by a frustrated owner. So all of the "homework" you do in preparation for your pup's arrival will benefit you both. The more informed and better prepared you are, the more you will know what to expect and the better equipped you will be to handle the ups and downs of raising a puppy. Hopefully, everyone in the household is willing to do his part in raising and caring for the pup. The anticipation of owning a dog often brings a lot of promises from excited family members: "I will walk him every day," "I will feed him," "I will house-train him," etc., but these things take time and effort, and promises can easily be forgotten once the novelty of the new pet has worn off.

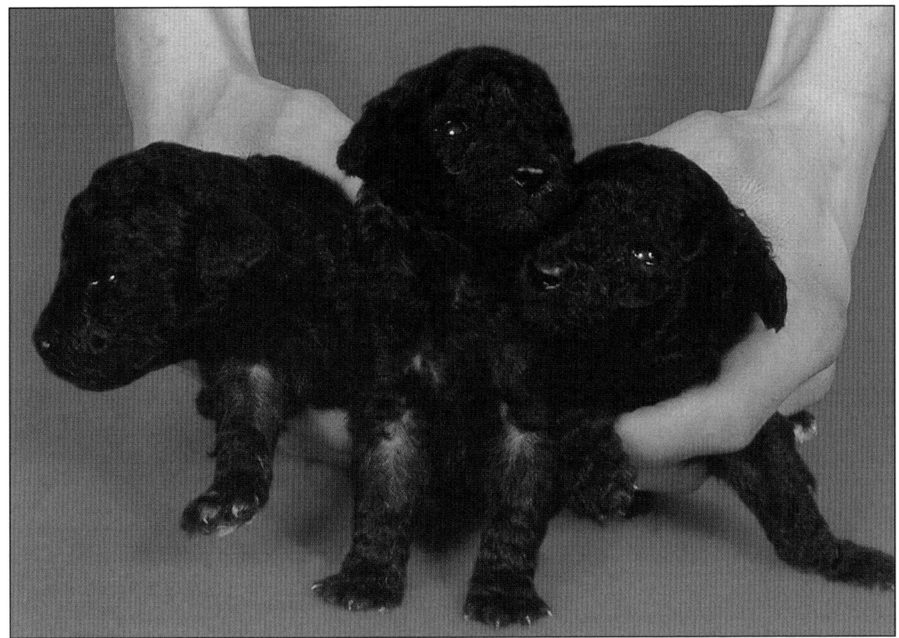

Selecting a breeder is as important as selecting your puppy. A healthy, sound pup of solid breeding gives you the best start in life with your new pet.

time of day or night. A reputable breeder will accept a puppy back, without questions, should you decide that this not the right dog for you.

When choosing a breeder, reputation is much more important than convenience of location. You may be well advised to avoid the novice who lives only a couple of miles away. The novice breeder, trying so hard to get rid of that first litter of puppies, is more than accommodating and anxious to sell you one. That breeder will charge you as much as any established breeder. The novice breeder isn't going to interrogate you and your family about your intentions with the puppy, the environment and time you can provide, etc. That breeder will be nowhere to be found when your Poodle pup becomes sick or acts inappropriately or aggressively in social settings. Socialization is a concern in every breed, and, with Poodles, it is vital to bring out the breed's natural affection for people.

Choosing a breeder is an important first step in dog ownership. Fortunately, the majority of Poodle breeders in all three varieties is devoted to the breed and its well-being. New owners should have little problem finding reputable breeders who are relatively nearby. The American Kennel Club is able to provide names of breeders, as can

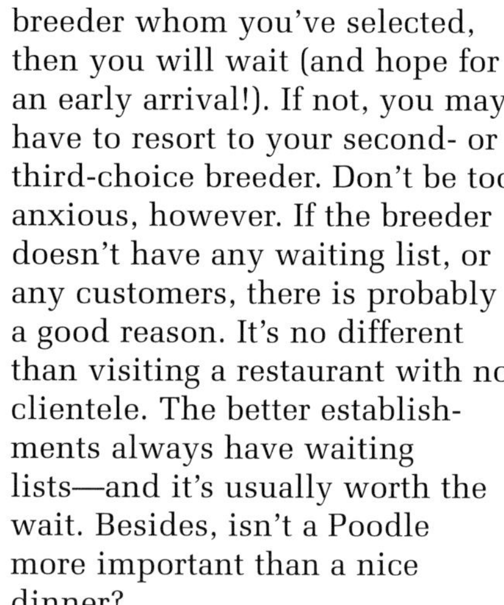

any local all-breed club or Poodle club. It's advisable to attend a dog show to see the Poodle strutting his pompons in the breed ring. Conformation shows are the best way to meet real Poodle people who can help you make contacts in the variety of your choice. Provided you approach the handlers when they are not terribly busy grooming their dogs, most are more than willing to answer questions, recommend breeders and give advice.

Once you have contacted and met a breeder or two and made your choice about which breeder is best suited to your needs, it's time to visit the litter. Keep in mind that many top breeders have waiting lists. Sometimes new owners have to wait as long as two years for a puppy. If you are really committed to the breeder whom you've selected, then you will wait (and hope for an early arrival!). If not, you may have to resort to your second- or third-choice breeder. Don't be too anxious, however. If the breeder doesn't have any waiting list, or any customers, there is probably a good reason. It's no different than visiting a restaurant with no clientele. The better establishments always have waiting lists—and it's usually worth the wait. Besides, isn't a Poodle more important than a nice dinner?

The gender of your puppy is largely a matter of personal taste, although there is a common belief among those who work with Poodles that bitches are quicker to learn and generally more loving and faithful. Males learn more slowly but retain the lesson longer.

Breeders commonly allow visitors to see the litter by around the fifth or sixth week, and puppies leave for their new homes between the eighth and tenth week. Some Toy Poodle breeders may keep their puppies even beyond the twelfth week. Breeders who permit their puppies to leave early are more interested in your money than in their puppies' well-being. Puppies need to learn the rules of the trade from their dams, and most dams continue teaching the pups manners and dos and

PUPPY SELECTION

Your selection of a good puppy can be determined by your needs. A show potential or a good pet? It is your choice. Every puppy, however, should be of good temperament. Although show-quality puppies are bred and raised with emphasis on physical conformation, responsible breeders strive for equally good temperament. Do not buy from a breeder who concentrates solely on physical beauty at the expense of personality.

Breeders rarely allow visitors to see the litter before the fifth week. These Poodle babies are too young for visitors.

don'ts until around the eighth week. Breeders spend significant amounts of time with the Poodle toddlers so that they are able to interact with the "other species," i.e., humans. Given the long history that dogs and humans have, bonding between the two species is natural but must be nurtured. A well-bred, well-socialized Poodle pup wants nothing more than to be near you and please you.

COMMITMENT OF OWNERSHIP

After considering all of these factors, you have most likely already made some very important decisions about selecting your puppy. You have chosen a variety of Poodle, which means that you have decided

PUPPY APPEARANCE

Your puppy should have a well-fed appearance but not a distended abdomen, which may indicate worms or incorrect feeding, or both. The body should be firm, with a solid feel. The skin of the abdomen should be pale pink and clean, without signs of scratching or rash. Dewclaws may be removed, so check to see if the breeder has had this done.

Handle with Care

You should be extremely careful about handling tiny puppies. Not that you might hurt them, but that the pups' mother may exhibit what is called "maternal aggression." It is a natural, instinctive reaction for the dam to protect her young against anything she interprets as predatory or possibly harmful to her pups. The sweetest, most gentle of bitches, after whelping a litter, often reacts this way, even to her owner.

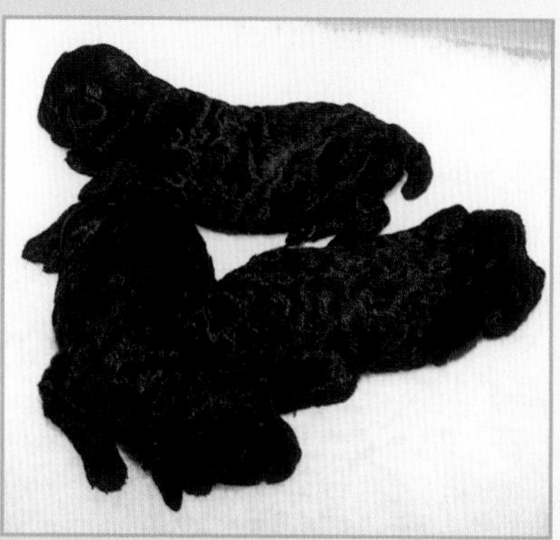

The breeder will not allow prospective owners to visit newborn puppies; he will usually start to allow visitors when the litter is around five weeks old. At this age, the puppies are still very small, especially Toy puppies. Pet the puppies gently and be very careful if holding them.

which characteristics you want in a dog and what type of dog will best fit into your family and lifestyle. If you have selected a breeder, you have gone a step further—you have done your research and found a responsible, conscientious person who breeds quality Poodles and who should be a reliable source of help as you and your puppy adjust to life together. If you have observed a litter in action, you have obtained a firsthand look at the dynamics of a puppy "pack" and, thus, you should have learned about each pup's individual personality—perhaps you have even found one that particularly appeals to you.

However, even if you have not yet found the Poodle puppy of your dreams, observing pups will help you learn to recognize certain behavior and to determine what a pup's behavior indicates about his temperament. You will be able to pick out which pups are the leaders, which ones are less outgoing, which ones are confident, which ones are shy, playful, friendly, aggressive, etc. Equally as important, you will learn to recognize what a healthy pup should look and act like. All of these things will help you in your search, and when you find the Poodle that was meant for you, you will know it!

Researching your breed, selecting a responsible breeder and observing as many pups as possible are all important steps on the way to dog ownership. It may seem like a lot of effort...and you have not even brought the pup home yet! Remember, though, you cannot be too careful when it comes to deciding on the type of dog you want and finding out about your prospective pup's background. Buying a puppy is not—or should not be—just

Time To Go Home

Breeders rarely release puppies until they are eight to ten weeks of age. This is an acceptable age for most breeds of dog, excepting Toy breeds, which are not released until around 12 weeks, given their petite sizes. If a breeder has a puppy that is 12 weeks or more, he is likely well socialized and housebroken. Be sure that he is otherwise healthy before deciding to take him home.

another whimsical purchase. This is one instance in which you actually do get to choose your own family! You may be thinking that buying a puppy should be fun—it should not be so serious and so much work. Keep in mind that your puppy is not a cuddly stuffed toy or decorative lawn ornament, but a creature that will become a real member of your family. You will come to realize that, while buying a puppy is a pleasurable and exciting endeavor, it is not something to be taken lightly. Relax...the fun will start when the pup comes home!

Always keep in mind that a puppy is nothing more than a baby in a furry disguise...a baby who is virtually helpless in a human world and who trusts his owner for fulfillment of his basic needs for survival. In addition to food, water and shelter, your pup needs care, protection, guidance and love. If you are not prepared to commit to this, then you are not prepared to own a dog.

The new owner continues the pup's training and socialization where the dam and breeder leave off.

ARE YOU A FIT OWNER?

If the breeder from whom you are buying a puppy asks you a lot of personal questions, do not be

insulted. Such a breeder wants to be sure that you will be a fit provider for his puppy.

"Wait a minute," you say. "How hard could this be? All of my neighbors own dogs and they seem to be doing just fine. Why should I have to worry about all of this?" Well, you should not worry about it; in fact, you will probably find that once your Poodle pup gets used to his new home, he will fall into his place in the family quite naturally. But it never hurts to emphasize the commitment of dog ownership. With some time and patience, it is really not too difficult to raise a curious and exuberant Poodle pup to become a well-adjusted and well-mannered adult dog—a dog that could be your most loyal friend.

PREPARING PUPPY'S PLACE IN YOUR HOME

Researching your breed and finding a breeder are only two aspects of the "homework" you will have to do before bringing your Poodle puppy home. You will also have to prepare your home and family for the new addition. Much as you would prepare a nursery for a newborn baby, you will need to designate a place in your home that will be the puppy's own. How you prepare your home will depend on how much freedom the dog will be allowed. Whatever you decide, you must ensure that he has a place that he can "call his own."

When you bring your new puppy into your home, you are bringing him into what will become his home as well. Obviously, you did not buy a puppy so that he could "rule the roost," but in order for a puppy to grow into a stable, well-adjusted dog, he has to feel comfortable in his surroundings. Remember, he is leaving the warmth and security of his mother and littermates, as well as the familiarity of the only place he has ever known, so it is important to make his transition as easy as possible. By preparing a place in your home for the puppy, you are making him feel as welcome as possible in a strange new place. It should not take him long to get used to it, but the sudden shock of being transplanted is somewhat traumatic for a young pup. Imagine how a small child would feel in the same situation—that is how your puppy must be feeling. It is up to you to reassure him and to let him know, "Little pup, you are going to like it here!"

WHAT YOU SHOULD BUY

CRATE

To someone unfamiliar with the use of crates in dog training, it may seem like punishment to shut a dog in a crate, but this is not the case at all. Most breeders and trainers recommend crates as the preferred tools for show puppies as well as pet puppies. Crates are not cruel—crates have many humane and highly effective uses in dog care and training. For example, crate training is a very popular and very successful house-breaking method. A crate can keep your dog safe during travel; and, perhaps most importantly, a crate provides your dog with a place of his own in your home. It serves as a "doggie bedroom" of sorts—your Poodle can curl up in his crate when he wants to sleep or when he just needs a break. Many dogs sleep in their crates overnight. With soft bedding and

YOUR SCHEDULE...

If you lead an erratic, unpredictable life, with daily or weekly changes in your work requirements, consider the problems of owning a puppy.

The new puppy has to be fed regularly, socialized (loved, petted, handled, introduced to other people) and, most importantly, allowed to visit outdoors for house-training. As the dog gets older, it can be more tolerant of deviations in its feeding and relief schedule.

PHOTO COURTESY OF DOSKOCIL.

Your local pet shop should be able to show you crates and kennels of various sizes and styles.

a favorite toy placed inside, a crate becomes a cozy pseudo-den for your dog. Like his ancestors, he too will seek out the comfort and retreat of a den—you just happen to be providing him with something a little more luxurious than what his early ancestors enjoyed.

As far as purchasing a crate,

CRATE-TRAINING TIPS

During crate training, you should partition off the section of the crate in which the pup stays. If he is given too big an area, this will hinder your

training efforts. Crate training is based on the fact that a dog does not like to soil his sleeping quarters, so it is ineffective to keep a pup in a crate that is so big that he can eliminate in one end and get far enough away from it to sleep. Also, you want to make the crate den-like for the pup. A blanket and a favorite toy will make the crate cozy for the small pup; as he grows, you may want to evict some of his "roommates" to make more room.

It will take some coaxing at first, but be patient. Given some time to get used to it, your pup will adapt to his new home-within-a-home quite nicely.

Crates are available in a wide range of sizes. The crate you choose should be comfortable for your Poodle at his full adult size.

the type that you buy is up to you. It will most likely be one of the two most popular types: wire or fiberglass. There are advantages and disadvantages to each type. For example, a wire crate is more open, allowing the air to flow through and affording the dog a view of what is going on around him, while a fiberglass crate is sturdier. Both can double as travel crates, providing protection for the dog. The size of the crate is another thing to consider. Puppies do not stay puppies forever—in fact, sometimes it seems as if they grow right before your eyes. Purchase a crate that will suit your Poodle at his adult size. Since there is such variance in the breed, discuss crate sizes with your breeder or a pet-supply store employee.

BEDDING

A soft mat or padding in the dog's crate will help the dog feel more at home. You may also like to provide a small blanket. This will take the place of the leaves, twigs, etc., that the pup would use in the wild to make a den; the pup can make his own "burrow" in the crate. Although your pup is far removed from his den-making ancestors, the denning instinct is still a part of his genetic makeup. Second, until you take your pup home, he has been sleeping amid the warmth of his mother and littermates, and while a blanket is not the same as a warm, breathing body, it still provides heat and something with which to snuggle. You will want to wash your pup's bedding frequently in case he has a potty accident in his crate, and replace

You must have a bed, bedding and a few chew toys ready for your Poodle puppy before he arrives at your home.

or remove any blanket that becomes ragged and starts to fall apart.

Toys

Toys are a must for dogs of all ages, especially for curious playful pups. Puppies are the "children" of the dog world, and what child does not love toys? Chew toys provide enjoyment to both dog and owner—your dog will enjoy playing with his favorite toys, while you will enjoy the fact that they distract him from your expensive shoes and leather couch. Puppies love to chew; in fact, chewing is a physical need for pups as they are teething, and everything looks appetizing! The full range of your possessions—from old dishrag to Oriental rug—are fair game in the eyes of a teething pup. Puppies are not all that discerning when it comes to finding something to literally "sink their teeth into"—everything tastes great!

Pet shops offer many kinds of toys suitable for the Poodle puppy. Never offer your Poodle any toy made for humans. Only use toys and chew devices made for dogs.

TOYS, TOYS, TOYS!

With a big variety of dog toys available, and so many that look like they would be a lot of fun for a dog, be careful in your selection. It is amazing what a set of puppy teeth can do to an innocent-looking toy; so, obviously, safety is a major consideration. Be sure to choose the most durable products that you can find. Hard nylon bones and toys are a safe bet, and many of them are offered in different scents and flavors that will be sure to capture your dog's attention. It is always fun to play a game of catch with your dog, and there are balls and flying discs that are specially made to withstand dog teeth.

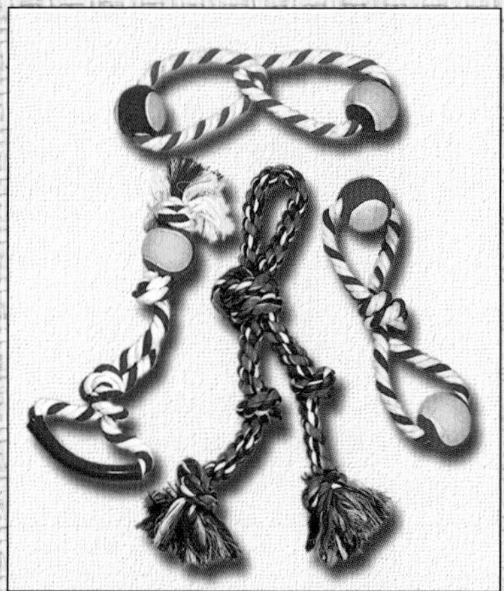

Poodle puppies should be offered the safest chew toys available. Breeders advise owners to resist stuffed toys, because they can become de-stuffed in no time. The overly excited pup may ingest the stuffing, which is neither nutritious nor digestible.

Similarly, squeaky toys are quite popular, but must be avoided for the Poodle. Perhaps a squeaky toy can be used as an aid in training, but not for free play. If a pup "disembowels" one of these, the small plastic squeaker inside can be dangerous if swallowed. Monitor the condition of all your pup's toys carefully and discard any that have been chewed to the point of becoming potentially dangerous.

Be careful of natural bones, which have a tendency to splinter into sharp, dangerous pieces. Also be careful of rawhide, which can turn into pieces that are easy to swallow or into a mushy mess on your carpet.

Leash

A nylon leash is probably the best option, as it is the most resistant to puppy teeth should your pup take a liking to chewing on his leash. Of course, this is a habit that should be nipped in the bud but, if your pup likes to chew on his leash, he has a very slim chance of being able to chew through the strong nylon. Nylon leashes are also lightweight, which is good for a young Poodle who is just getting used to the idea of walking on a leash. For everyday walking and safety purposes, the nylon leash is a good choice.

FINANCIAL RESPONSIBILITY

Grooming tools, collars, leashes, dog beds and, of course, toys will be expenses to you when you first obtain your pup, and the cost will

continue throughout your dog's lifetime. If your puppy damages or destroys your possessions (as most puppies surely will!) or something belonging to a neighbor, you can calculate additional expense. There is also flea and pest control, which every dog owner faces more than once. You must be able to handle the financial responsibility of owning a dog.

The BUCKLE COLLAR is the standard collar used for everyday purposes. Be sure that you adjust the buckle on growing puppies. Check it every day. It can become too tight overnight! These collars can be made of leather or nylon. Attach your dog's identification tags to this collar.

The CHOKE COLLAR is constructed of highly polished steel so that it slides easily through the stainless steel loop. The idea is that the dog controls the pressure around his neck and he will stop pulling if the collar becomes uncomfortable. It should be used *only* during training and is not appropriate for use on Toys and other small dogs.

The HALTER is for a trained dog that has to be restrained to prevent running away, chasing a cat and the like. Considered the most humane of all collars, it is frequently used on smaller dogs for which collars are not comfortable.

As your pup grows up and gets used to walking on the leash, you may want to purchase a flexible leash. These leashes allow you to extend the length to give the dog a broader area to explore or to shorten the length to keep the dog close to you. A Toy Poodle may be more comfortable using a harness for routine walks.

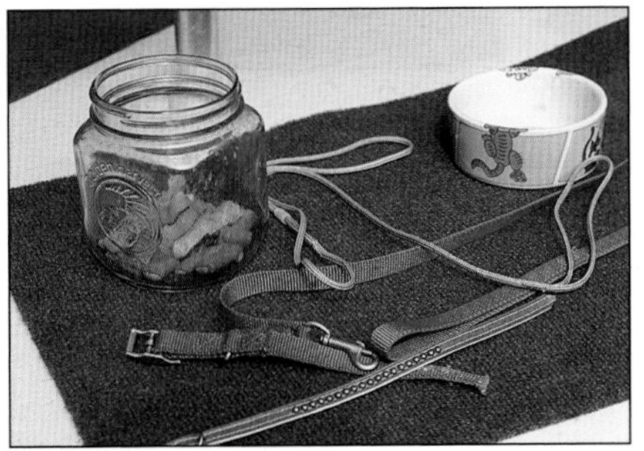

Collars, leashes, treats and food and water bowls are just a few of the things you will need before you bring the puppy home.

The collar and leash you select for your Poodle should be strong enough to restrain the dog, even if he attempts to pull and tug while walking.

COLLAR

Your pup should get used to wearing a collar all the time since you will want to attach his ID tags to it; plus, you have to attach the leash to something! A lightweight nylon collar is a good choice. Make sure that it fits snugly enough so that the pup cannot wriggle out of it, but is loose enough so that it will not be uncomfortably tight around the pup's neck. You should be able to fit a finger between the pup and the collar. It may take some time for your pup to get used to wearing the collar, but soon he will not even notice that it is there.

FOOD AND WATER BOWLS

Your pup will need two bowls, one for food and one for water. You may want two sets of bowls, one for inside and one for outside, depending on your Poodle's routine. Stainless steel or sturdy plastic bowls are popular choices. Plastic bowls are more chewable. Dogs tend not to chew on the steel variety, which can be sterilized. It is important to buy sturdy bowls since anything is in danger of

Pet shops sell bowls made from a variety of materials and in different sizes.

Choose durable, easily cleaned bowls for your Poodle.

PHOTO COURTESY OF MIKKI PET PRODUCTS.

being chewed by puppy teeth and you do not want your dog to be constantly chewing his bowl (for his safety and for your purse!). For a Standard Poodle, stands on which to elevate the dog's bowls serve as a bloat preventative.

CLEANING SUPPLIES

Until a pup is housebroken, you will be doing a lot of cleaning. "Accidents" will occur, which is okay in the beginning because the puppy does not know any better. All you can do is be prepared to clean up any accidents. Old rags, towels,

newspapers and a safe disinfectant are good to have on hand.

Beyond the Basics

The items previously discussed are the bare necessities. You will find out what else you need as you go along—grooming supplies, flea/tick protection, baby gates to partition a room, etc. These things will vary depending on your situation, but it is important that you have everything you need to feed and make your Poodle comfortable in his first few days at home.

NATURAL TOXINS

Examine your grass and garden landscaping before bringing your puppy home. Many varieties of plants have leaves, stems or

flowers that are toxic if ingested, and you can depend on a curious puppy to investigate them. Ask your veterinarian for information on poisonous plants or research them at your library.

If your Poodle is to have access to your yard, be sure it has not been treated with insecticides. Most lawn chemicals are deleterious to a dog's health.

PUPPY-PROOFING YOUR HOME

Aside from making sure that your Poodle will be comfortable in your home, you also have to make sure that your home is safe for your Poodle. This means taking precautions that your pup will not get into anything he should not get into and that there is nothing within his reach that may harm him should he sniff it, chew it, eat it, etc. This probably seems obvious since, while you are primarily concerned with your pup's safety, at the same time you do not want your belongings to be ruined. Breakables should be placed out of reach if your dog is to have full run of the house. If he is to be limited to certain places within the house, keep any potentially dangerous items in the "off-limits" areas. An electrical cord can pose a danger should the puppy decide to taste it—and who is going to convince a pup that it would not make a great chew toy? Cords should be fastened tightly against the wall. If your dog is going to spend time in a crate, make sure that there is nothing near his crate that he can reach if he sticks his curious little nose or paws through the openings. Just as you would with a child, keep all household cleaners and chemicals where the pup cannot get to them.

It is also important to make sure that the outside of your home is safe. Of course, your puppy should never be unsupervised, but a pup let loose in the yard will want to run and explore, and he should be granted that freedom. Do not let a fence give you a false sense of security; you would be surprised at how crafty (and persistent) a dog can be in working out how to dig under and

Your local pet shop sells tools to assist you in cleaning up after your dog.

PUPPY-PROOFING

Thoroughly puppy-proof your house before bringing your Poodle home. Never use roach or rodent poisons in any area accessible to

the dog. Avoid the use of toilet-bowl cleaners. Most dogs are born with toilet-bowl sonar and will take a drink if the lid is left open. Also keep the garbage secured and out of reach.

squeeze his way through small holes, or to jump or climb over a fence. The remedy is to make the fence high enough so that it really is impossible for your dog to get over it, and well embedded into the ground. Be sure to repair or secure any gaps in the fence. Check the fence periodically to ensure that it is in good shape and make repairs as needed; a very determined pup may return to the same spot to "work on it" until he is able to get through.

FIRST TRIP TO THE VET

You have picked out your puppy, and your home and family are ready. Now all you have to do is collect your Poodle from the breeder and the fun begins, right? Well...not so fast. Something else you need to arrange is your pup's first trip to the veterinarian. Perhaps the breeder can recommend someone in the area who specializes in Poodles, or maybe you know some other Poodle owners who can suggest a good vet. Either way, you should have an appointment arranged for your pup before you pick him up and plan on visiting the vet before (or very soon after) taking him home.

The pup's first visit will consist of an overall examination to make sure that the pup does not have any problems that are not apparent to you. The veterinarian will also set up a schedule for the pup's vaccinations; the breeder will inform you of which ones the pup has already received and the vet can continue from there.

INTRODUCTION TO THE FAMILY

Everyone in the house will be excited about the puppy's coming home and will want to pet him and play with him, but it is best to make the introduction low-key so as not to overwhelm the puppy. He is

MENTAL AND DENTAL

Toys not only help your puppy get the physical and mental stimulation he needs but also provide a great way to keep his teeth clean. Hard rubber or

nylon toys are designed to scrape away plaque. Soft toys are fun for a dog, but use caution as they are easily destructible.

Since your veterinarian will likely treat your Poodle for the dog's entire life, be certain that you are completely comfortable with your choice of vet.

apprehensive already. It is the first time he has been separated from his mother and the breeder, and the ride to your home is likely the first time he has been in a car. The last thing you want to do is smother him, as this will only frighten him further. This is not to say that human contact is not extremely necessary at this stage, because this is the time when a connection between the pup and his human family is formed. Gentle petting and soothing words should help console him, as well as just putting him down and letting him explore on his own (under your watchful eye, of course).

The pup may approach the family members or may busy himself with exploring for a while. Gradually, each person should spend some time with the pup, one at a time, crouching down to get as close to the pup's level as possible, and letting him sniff each person's hands and petting him gently. He definitely needs human attention and he needs to be touched—this is how to form an immediate bond. Just remember that the pup is

GRACE PERIOD

It will take at least two weeks for your puppy to become accustomed to his new surroundings. Give him

lots of love, attention, handling, frequent opportunities to relieve himself, a diet he likes to eat and a place he can call his own.

experiencing a lot of things for the first time, at the same time. There are new people, new noises, new smells and new things to investigate, so be gentle, be affectionate and be as comforting as you can be.

PUP'S FIRST NIGHT HOME

You have traveled home with your new charge safely in his crate. He's been to the vet for a thorough check-up; he's been weighed, his papers examined; perhaps he's even been vaccinated and wormed as well. He's met the family and he's licked the whole family, including the excited children and the less-than-happy cat. He's explored his area, his new bed, the yard and anywhere else he's been permitted. He's eaten his first meal at home and relieved himself in the proper place. He's heard lots of new sounds, smelled new friends and seen more of the outside world than ever before.

That was just the first day! He's worn out and is ready for bed…or so you think!

It's puppy's first night and you are ready to say "Good night"—keep in mind that this is the puppy's first night ever to be sleeping alone. His dam and littermates are no longer at paw's length and he's a bit scared, cold and lonely. Be reassuring to your new family member. This is not the time to spoil him and give in to his inevitable whining.

Puppies whine. They whine to let the others know where they are and hopefully to get company out of it. At bedtime, place your pup in his new bed or crate in his room and close the door. Mercifully, he may fall asleep without a peep. If the inevitable occurs, ignore the whining; he is fine. Be strong and keep his interest in mind. Do not allow your heart to become guilty and visit the pup. He will fall asleep.

Many breeders recommend placing a piece of bedding from

FOOD & TREATS

You will probably start feeding your pup the same food that he has been getting from the breeder; the breeder should give you a few days' supply to start you off.

Although you should not give your pup too many treats, you will want to have puppy treats on hand for coaxing, training, rewards, etc. Be careful, though, as a small pup's calorie requirements are relatively low and a few treats can add up to almost a full day's worth of calories without the required nutrition.

Your pup's exposure to other dogs is a vital part of his socialization. Do not let your Poodle meet strange dogs until he is completely vaccinated.

his former home in his new bed so that he recognizes the scent of his littermates. Others still advise placing a hot water bottle in his bed for warmth. This latter may be a good idea provided the pup doesn't attempt to suckle—he'll get good and wet and may not fall asleep so fast.

Puppy's first night can be somewhat stressful for the pup and his new family. Remember that you are setting the tone of nighttime at your house. Unless you want to play with your pup every night at 10 p.m., mid-night and 2 a.m., don't initiate the habit. Your family will thank you, and so will your pup!

PREVENTING PUPPY PROBLEMS

SOCIALIZATION

Now that you have done all of the preparatory work and have helped your pup get accustomed to his new home and family, it is about time for you to have some fun! Socializing your Poodle pup gives you the opportunity to show off your new friend, and your pup gets to reap the benefits of being an adorable furry creature that

PUP MEETS THE WORLD

Thorough socialization includes not only meeting new people but also being introduced to new experiences

such as riding in the car, having his coat brushed, hearing the television, walking in a crowd—the list is endless. The more your pup experiences, and the more positive the experiences are, the less of a shock and the less scary it will be for your pup to encounter new things.

people will want to pet and, in general, think is absolutely precious!

Besides getting to know his new family, your puppy should be exposed to other people, animals and situations. This will help him become well adjusted as he grows up and less prone to being timid or fearful of the new things he will encounter. Of course, he must not come into close contact with dogs you don't know well until his course of injections is complete.

Your pup's socialization began at the breeder's, but now it is your responsibility to continue it. The socialization he receives up until the age of 12 weeks is the most critical, as this is the time when he forms his impressions of the outside world. Be especially careful during the eight-to-ten-week-old period, also known as the fear period, during which you may be bringing your Poodle home. The interaction he receives during this time should be gentle and reassuring. Lack of socialization can manifest itself in fear and aggression as the dog grows up. He needs lots of human contact, affection, handling and exposure to other animals.

Once your pup has received his necessary vaccinations, feel free to take him out and about (on his leash, of course). Walk him around the neighborhood, take him on your daily errands, let people pet him, let him meet

Training Tip

Training your Poodle takes much patience, but with such a trainable breed, you should soon see results from your efforts. If you have a puppy that seems untrainable, take him to a trainer or behaviorist. The dog may have a personality problem that requires the help of a professional, or perhaps you need help in learning how to train your dog.

other dogs and pets, etc. Puppies do not have to try to make friends; there will be no shortage of people who will want to introduce themselves. Just make sure that you carefully supervise each meeting. If the neighborhood children want to say hello, for example, that is great—children and pups most often make great companions. However, sometimes an excited child can unintentionally handle a pup too roughly, or an overzealous pup can playfully nip a little too hard. You want to make socialization experiences positive ones. What a pup learns during this very formative stage will impact his attitude toward future encounters. You want your dog to be comfortable around everyone. A pup that has a bad

FENCE ME IN!

Poodles love to be near their owners and to be part of the action. So feel free to invite your

dog to join in the fun, while ensuring his safety, of course. Wire pens, known as ex-pens, are easily portable so that you can bring your Poodle along and provide him with a place of safe confinement wherever you go.

experience with a child may grow up to be a dog that is shy around or aggressive toward children.

Consistency in Training

Dogs, being pack animals, naturally need a leader, or else they try to establish dominance in their packs. When you bring a dog into your family, the choice of who becomes the leader and who becomes the "pack" is entirely up to you! Your pup's instinctive quest for dominance, coupled with the fact that it is nearly impossible to look at an adorable Poodle pup with his "puppy-dog" eyes and not cave in, give the pup almost an unfair advantage in getting the upper hand!

A pup will definitely test the waters to see what he can and cannot do. Do not give in to those pleading eyes—stand your ground when it comes to disciplining the pup and make sure that all family members do the same. It will only confuse the pup when Mother tells him to get off the couch when he is used to sitting up there with Father to watch the evening news. Avoid discrepancies by having all members of the household decide on the rules before the pup even comes home...and be consistent in enforcing them! Early training shapes the dog's personality, so you cannot be unclear in what you expect.

COMMON PUPPY PROBLEMS

The best way to prevent puppy problems is to be proactive in stopping an undesirable behavior as soon as it starts. The old saying "You can't teach an old dog new tricks" does not necessarily hold true, but it is true that it is much easier to discourage bad behavior in a young developing pup than to wait until the pup's bad behavior becomes the adult dog's bad habit. There are some problems that are especially prevalent in puppies as they develop.

Nipping

As puppies start to teethe, they feel the need to sink their teeth into anything available...unfortunately that includes your fingers, arms, hair and toes. You may find this behavior cute for the first five seconds...until you feel just how sharp those puppy teeth are. This is something you want to discourage immediately and consistently with a firm "No!" (or whatever number of firm "Nos" it takes for him to understand that you mean business). Then replace your finger with an appropriate chew toy. While this behavior is merely annoying when the dog is young, it can become dangerous as your Poodle's adult teeth grow in and his jaws develop, and he continues to think it is okay to gnaw on human appendages. Your Poodle does not mean any harm with a friendly nip, but he also does not know his own strength.

Crying/Whining

Your pup will often cry, whine, whimper, howl or make some other type of commotion when he is left alone. This is basically his way of calling out for attention to make sure that you know he is there and that you have not forgotten about him. He feels insecure when he is left alone, when you are out of the house

CHEWING TIPS

Chewing goes hand in hand with nipping in the sense that a teething puppy is always looking for a way to soothe his aching gums. In this case, instead of chewing on you, he may have taken a liking to your favorite shoe or something else that he should not be chewing. Again, realize that this is a normal canine behavior that does not need to be discouraged, only redirected. Your pup just needs to be taught what is acceptable to chew on and what is off limits. Consistently tell him "No" when you catch him chewing on something forbidden and give him a chew toy. Conversely, praise him when you catch him chewing on something appropriate. In this way, you are discouraging the inappropriate behavior and reinforcing the desired behavior. The puppy's chewing should stop after his adult teeth have come in, but an adult dog continues to chew for various reasons—perhaps because he is bored, needs to relieve tension or just likes to chew. That is why it is important to redirect his chewing when he is still young.

Poodles tend to be gregarious with other dogs if properly socialized from an early age. This Miniature Poodle has a brawny protector in his black and tan companion.

and he is in his crate or when you are in another part of the house and he cannot see you. The noise he is making is an expression of the anxiety he feels at being alone, so he needs to be taught that being alone is okay. You are not actually training the dog to stop making noise, you are training him to feel comfortable when he is alone and thus removing the need for him to make the noise. This is where the crate with cozy bedding and a toy comes in handy. You want to know that he is safe when you are not there to supervise, and you know that he will be safe in his crate rather than roaming freely about the house. In order for the pup to stay in his crate without making a fuss, he needs to be comfortable in his crate. On that note, it is extremely important that the crate is never used as a form of punishment, or the pup will have a negative association with the crate.

Accustom the pup to the crate in short, gradually increasing time intervals in which you put him in the crate, maybe with a treat, and stay in the room with him. If he cries or makes a fuss, do not go to him, but stay in his sight. Gradually he will realize that staying in his crate is all right without your help, and it will not be so traumatic for him when you are not around. You may want to leave the radio on softly when you leave the house; the sound of human voices may be comforting to him.

PUPPY PROBLEMS

The majority of problems that is commonly seen in young pups will disappear as your dog gets older. However, how you deal with problems when he is young will determine how he reacts to discipline as an adult dog. It is important to establish who is boss (hopefully it will be you!) right away when you are first bonding with your dog. This bond will set the tone for the rest of your life together.

EVERYDAY CARE OF YOUR

POODLE

DIETARY AND FEEDING CONSIDERATIONS

Today the choices of food for your Poodle are many and varied. There are simply dozens of brands of food in all sorts of flavors and textures, ranging from puppy diets to those for seniors. There are even hypoallergenic and low-calorie diets available. Because your Poodle's food has a bearing on coat, health and temperament, it is essential that the most suitable diet is selected for a Poodle of his age. It is fair to say, however, that even dedicated owners can be somewhat perplexed by the enormous range of foods available. Only understanding what is best for your dog will help you reach an informed decision.

Dog foods are produced in three basic types: dry, semi-moist and canned. Dry foods tend to be less expensive than semi-moist and canned. These contain the least fat and the most preservatives. In general, canned foods are made up of 60–70 percent water, while semi-moist ones often contain so much sugar that they are perhaps the least preferred by owners, even though their dogs seem to like them.

When selecting your dog's diet, three stages of development must be considered: the puppy stage, the adult stage and the senior stage.

STORING FOOD

You must store your dry dog food carefully. Open packages of dog food quickly lose their vitamin value, usually within 90 days of being opened. Mold

spores and vermin could also contaminate the food. Seal the bag tightly or store the food in an airtight container.

Puppies are born with the instinct to suck milk from their mother's teats; they should suckle for about six weeks before being completely weaned.

PUPPY STAGE

Puppies instinctively want to suck milk from their mother's teats and a normal puppy will exhibit this behavior from just a few moments following birth. If puppies do not attempt to suckle within the first half-hour or so, they should be encouraged to do so. This early milk supply is important in providing colostrum to protect the puppies during the first eight to ten weeks of their lives. Although a mother's milk is much better than any milk formula, despite there being some excellent ones available, if the puppies do not feed, the breeder will have to feed them himself. For those with less experience, advice from a veterinarian is important so that not only the right quantity of milk is fed but also that of correct quality, fed at suitably frequent intervals, usually every two hours during the first few days of life.

Puppies should be allowed to nurse from their mothers for about the first six weeks, although from the third or fourth week the breeder will begin to introduce small portions of suitable solid food. Most breeders like to introduce alternate milk and meat

CAUTION

You should be careful where you exercise your dog. Many countryside areas have been sprayed with chemicals that are highly toxic to both dogs and humans. Never allow your dog to eat grass or drink from puddles on either public or private grounds, as the run-off water may contain chemicals from sprays and herbicides.

meals initially, building up to weaning time.

By the time the puppies are seven or a maximum of eight weeks old, they should be fully weaned and fed solely on a proprietary puppy food. Selection of the most suitable, good-quality diet at this time is essential, for a puppy's fastest growth rate is during the first year of life. Veterinarians are usually able to offer advice in this regard. The frequency of meals will be reduced until eventually the puppy is switched to an adult food.

Puppy and junior diets should be well balanced for the needs of your dog so that, except in certain circumstances, additional vitamins, minerals and proteins will not be required.

Adult Diets

A dog is considered an adult when he has stopped growing, which will vary depending on the variety of Poodle. Standards take up to 18 months to mature; Minis about 12 months; and Toys 6 to 8 months. Again you should rely upon your veterinarian, breeder or dietary specialist to recommend an acceptable maintenance diet and advise you on the proper age to switch to adult food. Major dog food manufacturers specialize in this type of food, and it is just necessary for you to select the one best suited to your dog's needs. Active dogs may have different requirements than sedate dogs.

FOOD PREFERENCE

Selecting the best dry dog food is difficult. There is no majority consensus among veterinary scientists as to the value of nutrient analyses (protein, fat, fiber, moisture, ash, cholesterol, minerals, etc.). All agree that feeding trials are what matter, but you also have to consider the

individual dog. Its weight, age and activity level, and what pleases its taste, all must be considered. It is probably best to take the advice of your veterinarian. Every dog's dietary requirements vary, even during the lifetime of a particular dog.

If your dog is fed a good dry food, it does not require supplements of meat or vegetables. Dogs do appreciate a little variety in their diets, so you may choose to stay with the same brand but vary the flavor. Alternatively, you may wish to add a little flavored stock to give a difference to the taste.

Senior Diets

As dogs get older, their metabolism changes. The older dog usually exercises less, moves more slowly and sleeps more. This change in lifestyle and physiological performance requires a change in diet. Since

FEEDING TIPS

Dog food must be served at room temperature, neither too hot nor too cold. Fresh water, changed often and served in a clean bowl, is mandatory, especially when feeding dry food.

Dogs must chew their food. Hard pellets are excellent; these can be mixed with a moist food.

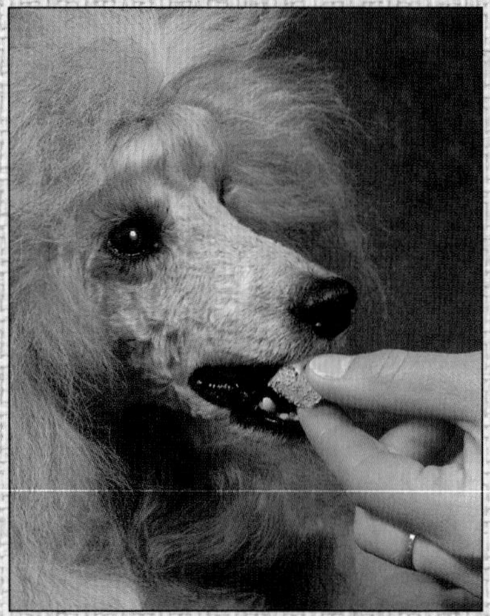

Never feed your dog from the table while you are eating. Never feed your dog leftovers from your own meal. They usually contain too much fat and too much seasoning. Don't add leftovers or any extras to normal dog food. The normal food is usually balanced and adding something extra destroys the balance. Except for age-related changes, dogs do not require dietary variations. They can be fed the same diet, day after day, without their becoming bored or ill.

these changes take place slowly, they might not be recognizable. What is easily recognizable is weight gain. By continuing to feed your dog an adult-maintenance diet when he is slowing down metabolically, your dog will gain weight. Obesity in an older dog compounds the health problems that already accompany old age.

As your dog gets older, few of his organs function up to par. The kidneys slow down and the intestines become less efficient. These age-related factors are best handled with a change in diet and a change in feeding schedule to give smaller portions that are more easily digested.

There is no single best diet for every older dog. While many dogs do well on light or senior diets, other dogs do better on puppy diets or other special premium diets such as lamb and rice. Be sensitive to your senior Poodle's diet and this will help control other problems that may arise with your old friend.

WATER

Just as your dog needs proper nutrition from his food, water is an essential "nutrient" as well. Water keeps the dog's body properly hydrated and promotes normal function of the body's systems. During housebreaking, it is necessary to keep an eye on how much water your Poodle is drinking but, once he is reliably

A Worthy Investment

Veterinary studies have proven that a balanced high-quality diet pays off in your dog's coat quality, behavior and activity level. Invest in premium brands for the maximum benefit for your dog.

GRAIN-BASED DIETS

Some less expensive dog foods are based on grains and other plant proteins. While these products may appear to be attractively priced, many breeders prefer a diet based

on animal proteins and believe that they are more conducive to your dog's health. Many grain-based diets rely on soy protein that may cause flatulence (passing gas).

There are many cases, however, when your dog might require a special diet. These special requirements should only be recommended by your veterinarian.

trained, he should have access to clean fresh water at all times. Make sure that the dog's water bowl is clean, and change the water often, making sure that water is always available for your dog, especially if you feed dry food.

EXERCISE

Although most Poodles today do not enjoy the rigors of retrieving fallen fowl from a rowdy river, the breed still requires some form of exercise. A sedentary lifestyle is as harmful to a Poodle as it is to a person.

The Standard Poodle requires more structured exercise than his smaller counterparts. Miniatures and Toys tend to exercise themselves more so than Standards who need more space to stretch their legs. Regular walks, play sessions in the yard and letting the dog run free in the yard under your supervision are sufficient forms of exercise for the Poodle. For those who are more ambitious, you will find that your Poodle also enjoys long walks (appropriate to his size), an occasional hike or, best of all, a swim!

Bear in mind that an overweight dog should never be suddenly over-exercised; instead, he should be allowed to increase exercise slowly. Not only is exercise essential to keep the dog's body fit, it is essential to his mental well-being. A bored dog will find something to do, which often manifests itself in some type of destructive behavior. In this sense, it is essential for the owner's mental well-being as well!

GROOMING THE POODLE

To begin, Poodles should be groomed on a table or bench, never

Poodles, like humans, require activity to keep their muscles in tone. As descendants of water retrievers, Poodles are excellent fetching dogs and easily can be exercised with retrieving games.

Your local pet shop should have a full range of grooming tools with which you can properly groom your Poodle.

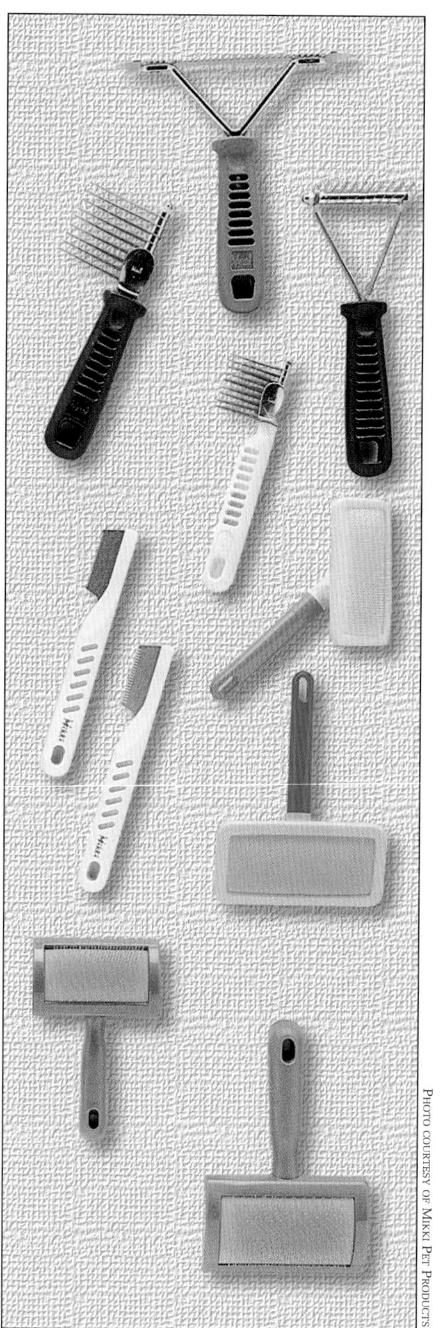

PHOTO COURTESY OF MIKKI PET PRODUCTS.

on the floor. The dog quickly learns to associate the table with grooming, and he looks forward to the attention he will receive during the short daily brushing and the biscuit treat he'll receive when the process is finished.

Bathe the dog once a week and brush the coat every other day to keep it free of mats and foreign matter. This method is quite easy with a Toy or Miniature because the dog is small and the amount of coat is not excessive. On a Standard, however, this bathing and brushing can take up to several hours due to drying time. The heavier the coat and the longer the hair, the more work will be involved in bathing

GROOMING EQUIPMENT

How much grooming equipment you purchase will depend on how much grooming you are going to do. Here are some basics:

- Slicker brush
- Metal comb
- Scissors
- Electric clipper
- Rubber mat
- Dog shampoo
- Spray hose attachment
- Towels
- Hair dryer
- Ear cleaner
- Cotton balls
- Nail clippers

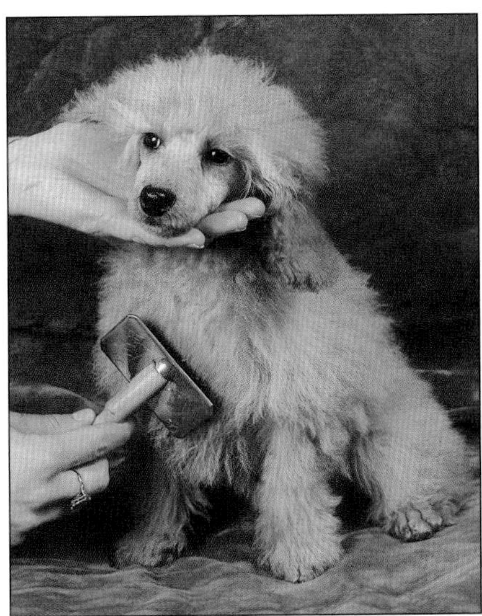

You need a stiff wire brush (slicker brush) for the routine brushing of your Poodle's coat.

When all the hair in your left hand is brushed out, you can check your work with the comb. There should be no mats or knots in the hair as you run the comb through it.

Work your way forward to include brushing the topknot and ears. Next, brush the leg hair from the foot end to the body end of the leg.

Brushing too much hair at one time prevents you from doing a thorough job and will leave knots

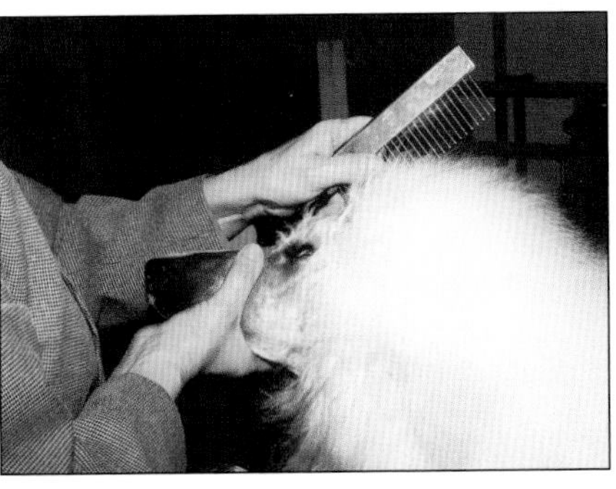

After a thorough brushing, you should be able to comb through the coat without any mats or tangles.

and brushing it dry. You will need a heavy-duty electric hair dryer to accomplish this task.

Brushing

To brush your Poodle correctly, you will need a stiff wire brush called a slicker brush. A metal comb is also needed. Begin brushing at the tail end of the dog and brush the hair toward the head. Hold the brush in your right hand and a section of hair in your left hand. (For left-handed people, you must reverse this position.) Now, with the brush, pull a line of hair out of your left hand so that you can see a definite line of scalp between the brushed hair and the unbrushed hair. This is called line brushing and it is the only way to brush a dog's hair to assure that the coat will be free of mats and knots.

untouched within the hair. That's why line brushing is so important and successful.

Always brush the dog thoroughly before bathing the dog. If knotted hair gets wet, it will create bigger knots than when it is dry. Once the coat is brushed, then you can bathe the dog.

Bathing

Only use a dog shampoo for bathing your Poodle. Human shampoo dries out the hair too much and can cause skin problems in dogs. Wet the dog, then apply the shampoo and rub it into a lather just as you do when you shampoo your own hair.

Rinse thoroughly to remove all shampoo. Leaving a residue of chemicals can cause major harm to hair and skin, so be sure that the hair is rinsed well with warm water.

SOAP IT UP

The use of human soap products like shampoo, bubble bath and hand soap can be damaging to a dog's coat and skin. Human products are too strong and remove the protective oils

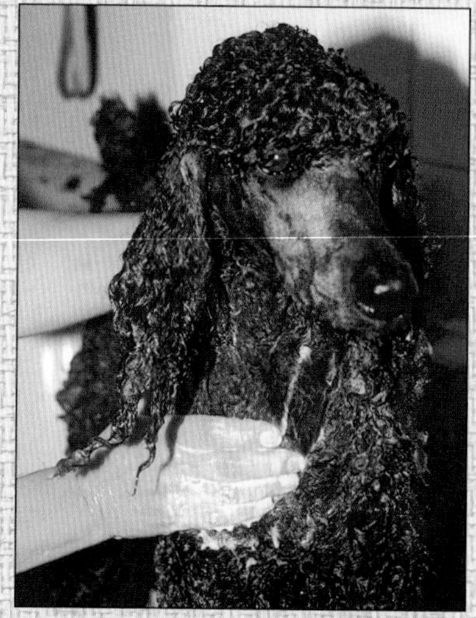

coating the dog's hair and skin (that make him water-resistant). Use only shampoo made especially for dogs and you may like to use a medicated shampoo, which will help to keep external parasites at bay.

Towel-dry the coat after the final rinsing. Following that, you can air-dry the coat, but you must keep the dog out of cold air and drafts until he's completely dry. You may choose to dry the coat with the hair dryer, in which case you'll find that the end result is a fluffier and fuller coat with less kinky curls than an air-dried coat.

In either case, the final step will be another turn at brushing out the coat for that finished well-groomed look. When a professional grooms a Poodle, he or she does all of the final sculpting and scissoring after that final brush-out. A groomer never scissors a dirty coat.

Clipping and Trimming

The professional groomer will style the coat according to your directions. He or she will scissor the hair on the body to a manageable length for you to keep nicely at home. The groomer will also shave the face, feet and base of tail as well as any other sections of the body that call for shaving according to the style you've chosen.

If you are planning on learning how to clip and trim your Poodle, you must expect to invest some money in good tools. An electric clipper and several different-sized blades will be necessary as well as different-sized shears. Before you purchase these items, be guided by

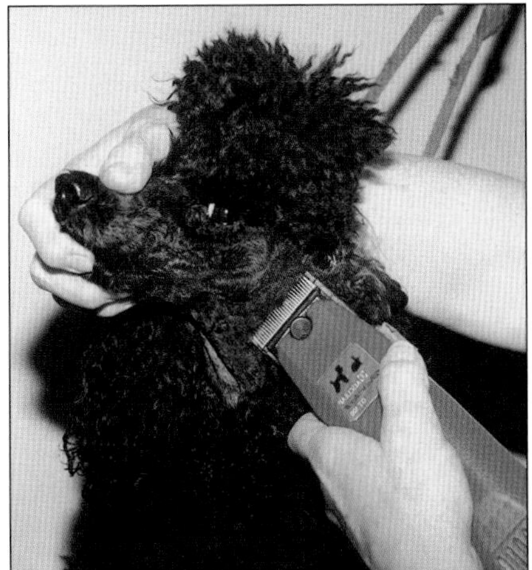

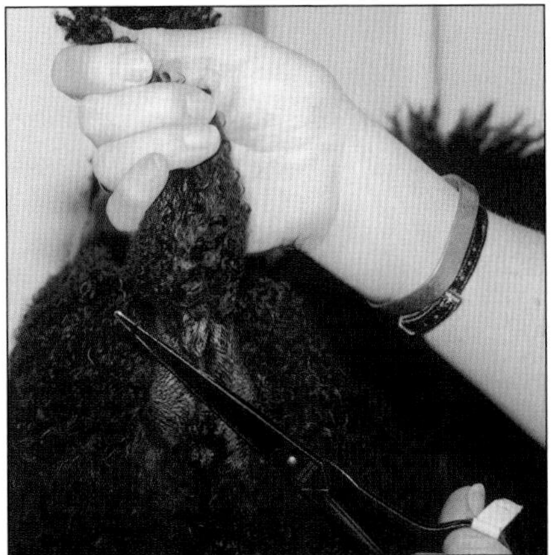

the person who will teach you how to groom. It pays in the long run to buy quality equipment the first time.

Ear Cleaning

The ears should be kept clean and any excess hair inside the ear

BATHING BEAUTY

Once you are sure that the dog is thoroughly rinsed, squeeze the excess water out of the coat with your hand and dry him with a heavy

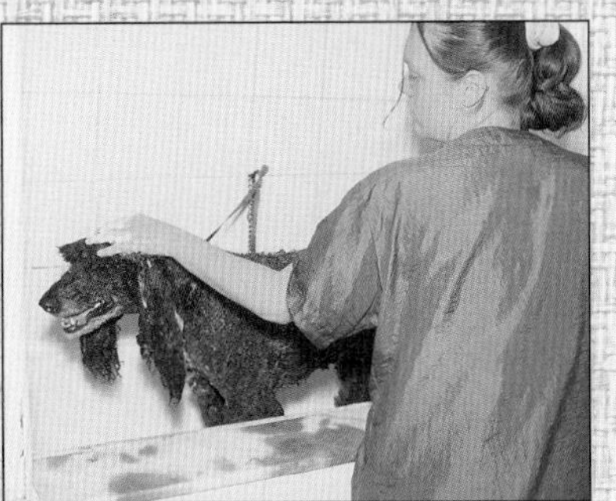

towel. You may choose to use a hair dryer on his coat or just let it dry naturally. In cold weather, never allow your dog outside with a wet coat.

There are "dry bath" products on the market, which are sprays and powders intended for spot cleaning that can be used between regular baths, if necessary. They are not substitutes for regular baths, but they are easy to use for touch-ups as they do not require rinsing.

Grooming a Poodle requires skill and patience. Whether your Poodle will be clipped in the pet style or groomed for the show ring, he will require proper training to endure the procedure. Most Poodles inherit a natural tolerance for the grooming salon.

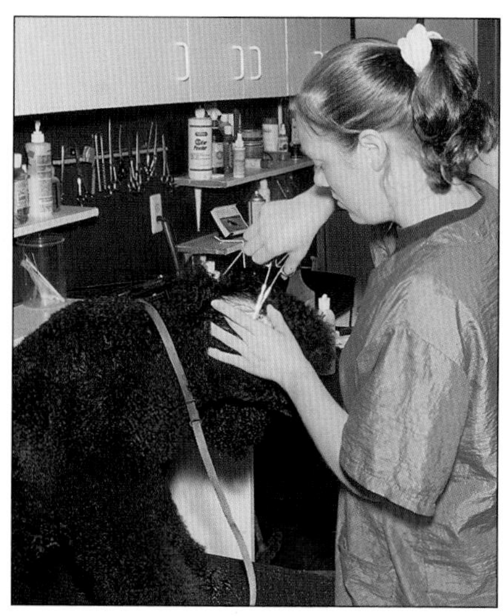

Top, left: Drying and brushing during the last stages of grooming. Top, right: A Poodle's ears require special attention. Take instruction in ear care from your professional groomer or your vet.

Poodles are most often groomed on a table. This allows the groomer more control and less stress on her own body.

should be carefully plucked out. Ears can be cleaned with a cotton ball and ear powder made especially for dogs. Be on the lookout for any signs of infection or ear-mite infestation. If your

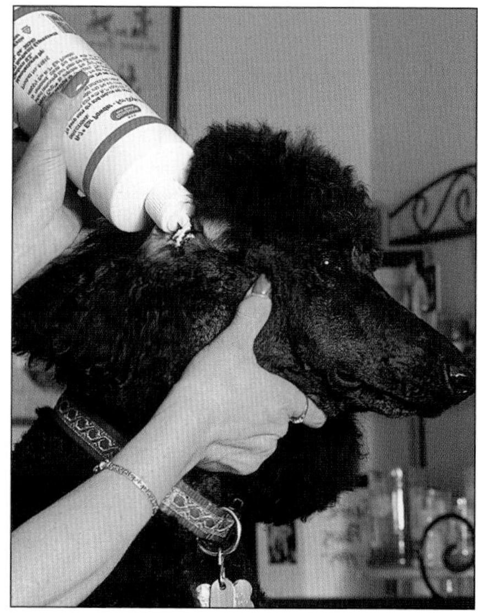

Bottom, left: More Poodles should be named "Job." Consider the patience that a Poodle needs to endure a two- or three-hour grooming session. Bottom, right: Your local pet shop probably has a special cleanser with which to treat your Poodle's ears every time the dog is bathed.

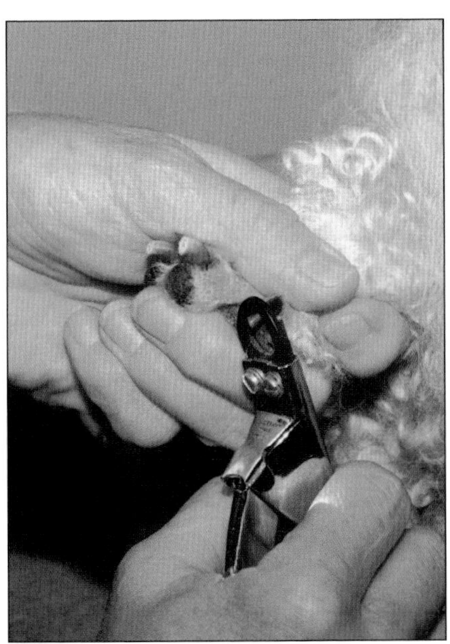

The Poodle's nails should be clipped with nail clippers made for dogs.

Poodle has been shaking his head or scratching at his ears frequently, this usually indicates a problem. If his ears have an unusual odor, this is a sure sign of mite infestation or infection, and a signal to have his ears checked by the veterinarian.

Nail Clipping

Your Poodle should be accustomed to having his nails trimmed at an early age, since it will be part of your maintenance routine throughout his life. Not only does it look nicer, but long nails can scratch someone unintentionally. Also, a long nail has a better chance of ripping and bleeding, or of causing the feet to spread. A good rule of thumb is that if you can hear your dog's nails' clicking on the floor when he walks, his nails are too long.

Before you start cutting, make sure you can identify the "quick" in each nail. The quick is a blood vessel that runs through the center of each nail and grows rather close to the end. It will

PEDICURE TIP

A dog that spends a lot of time outside on a hard surface, such as cement or pavement, will have his nails naturally worn down and may not

need to have them trimmed as often, except maybe in the colder months when he is not outside as much. Regardless, it is best to get your dog accustomed to this procedure at an early age so that he is used to it. Some dogs are especially sensitive about having their feet touched, but if a dog has experienced it since he was young, he should not be bothered by it.

With black or dark nails, it's best to clip only the tip of the nail or to use a file.

In light-colored nails, clipping is much simpler because you can see the vein (or quick) that grows inside the casing.

bleed if accidentally cut, which will be quite painful for the dog as it contains nerve endings. Keep some type of clotting agent on hand, such as a styptic pencil or styptic powder (the type used for shaving). This will stop the bleeding quickly when applied to the end of the cut nail. Do not panic if this happens, just stop the bleeding and talk soothingly to your dog. Once he has calmed down, move on to the next nail. It is better to clip a little at a time, particularly with black-nailed dogs.

Hold your pup steady as you begin trimming his nails; you do not want him to make any sudden movements or run away. Talk to him soothingly and stroke him as you clip. Holding his foot in your hand, simply take off the end of each nail in one quick clip. You can purchase nail clippers that are specially made for dogs; you can probably find them wherever you buy pet or grooming supplies.

TRAVELING WITH YOUR DOG

Car Travel

You should accustom your Poodle to riding in a car at an early age. You may or may not take him in the car often, but at the very least he will need to go to the vet and you do not want these trips to be traumatic for the dog or troublesome to ride in the car is in his crate. If he uses a

Your Poodle(s) must be transported in a crate, both for your safety and the safety of the dog. If your dog is crate trained from a young age, he will accept the crate no matter where he is.

crate in the house, you can use the same crate for travel.

Put the pup in the crate and see how he reacts. If he seems uneasy, you can have a passenger hold him on his lap while you drive. Another option is a specially made safety harness for dogs, which straps the dog in much like a seat belt. Do not let the dog roam loose in the vehicle—this is very dangerous! If you should stop short, your dog can be thrown and injured. If the dog starts climbing on you and pestering you while you are driving, you will not be able to concentrate on the road. It is an unsafe situation for everyone—human and canine.

For long trips, be prepared to

RESTRICTED PARKING

Never leave your dog alone in the car. In hot weather, your dog can die from the high temperature inside a closed vehicle; even a car parked in the shade

can heat up very quickly. Leaving the window open is dangerous as well since the dog can hurt himself trying to get out.

Your Poodle's education does *not* include driving lessons! Safety is your main concern when traveling with your Poodle.

stop to let the dog relieve himself. Bring along whatever you need to clean up after him. You should take along some paper towels and perhaps some old bath towels for use should he have an accident in the car or suffer from motion sickness.

Air Travel

Contact your chosen airline before proceeding with travel plans that include your Poodle. The dog will be required to travel in a fiberglass crate and you should always check in advance with the airline regarding specific requirements. On many airlines, small pets whose crates fall within the specified size limitations are granted "carry-on" status and can accompany their owners in the cabin, in their crates. This should be the case with a Toy Poodle; again, check with the airline ahead of time.

To help put the dog at ease, give him one of his favorite toys in the crate. Do not feed the dog for several hours prior to checking in so that you minimize his need to relieve himself. For long trips, you will have to include food and

ON THE ROAD

If you are going on a long car trip with your dog, be sure the hotels are dog-friendly. Many hotels do not accept dogs. Also take along

some cold water or some ice that can be thawed and offered to your dog if he becomes overheated. Most dogs like to lick ice.

Look around for places in which you can board your Poodle should the need arise. You want a boarding kennel that is roomy, clean and convenient. Usually your vet can suggest a suitable facility with an established reputation.

water bowls in the dog's crate, and a portion of food, so that airline employees can tend to the dogs between legs of the trip.

Make sure your dog is properly identified and that your contact information appears on his ID tags and on his crate. If not permitted in the cabin, your Poodle will travel in a different area of the plane than the human passengers, so every rule must be strictly followed to prevent the risk of getting separated from your dog—or worse!

ON-LEAD ONLY

When traveling, never let your dog off-lead in a strange area. Your dog could run away out of fear, decide to chase a passing squirrel or cat or simply want to stretch his legs without restriction—if any of these happen, you might never see your canine friend again. Proper training and identification will pay off should you find you and your Poodle in this situation.

BOARDING

So you want to take a family vacation—and you want to include *all* members of the family. You would probably make arrangements for accommodations ahead of time anyway, but this is especially important when traveling with a dog. You do not want to make an overnight stop at the only place around for miles and find out that they do not allow dogs. Also, you do not want to reserve a room for your family without confirming that you are traveling with a dog, because, if it is against their policy, you may not have a place to stay.

Alternatively, if you are traveling and choose not to bring your Poodle, you will have to make arrangements for him while you are away. Some options are to take him to a neighbor's house to stay while you are gone, to have a trusted neighbor stop by often or stay at your house or to bring your dog to a reputable boarding kennel. If you choose to board him at a kennel, you should visit in advance to see the facilities provided, how clean they are and where the dogs are kept. Talk to some of the employees and see how they treat the dogs—do they spend time with the dogs, play with them, exercise them, groom them, etc.? Also find out the kennel's policy on vaccinations and what they require. This is for all of the dogs' safety, since when dogs are kept together, there is a greater risk of diseases being passed from dog to dog.

COLLAR REQUIRED

If your dog gets lost, he is not able to ask for directions home. Identification tags securely fastened to the collar give important information—the dog's name, the owner's name,

the owner's address and a telephone number where the owner can be reached. This makes it easy for whoever finds the dog to contact the owner and arrange to have the dog returned. An added advantage is that a person will be more likely to approach a lost dog who has ID tags on his collar; it tells the person that this is somebody's pet rather than a stray. This is the easiest and fastest method of identification, provided that the tags stay on the collar and the collar stays on the dog.

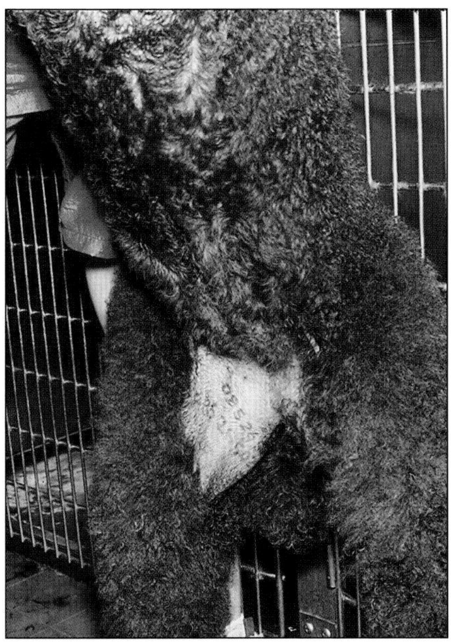

A Poodle tattooed on the inside of his thigh.

IDENTIFICATION

Your Poodle is your valued companion and friend. That is why you always keep a close eye on him and you have made sure that he cannot escape from the yard or wriggle out of his collar and run away from you. However, accidents can happen and there may come a time when your dog unexpectedly gets separated from you. If this unfortunate event should occur, the first thing on your mind will be finding him. Proper identification, including an ID tag, a tattoo and possibly a microchip, will increase the chances of his being returned to you safely and quickly.

IDENTIFICATION OPTIONS

As puppies become more and more expensive, especially those puppies of high quality for showing and/or breeding, they have a greater chance of being stolen. The usual collar and dog tag are, of course, easily removed. But there are two permanent techniques that have become widely used for identification.

The puppy microchip implantation involves the injection of a small microchip, about the size of a corn kernel, under the skin of the dog. If your dog shows up at a clinic or shelter, or is offered for resale under less than savory circumstances, it can be positively identified by the microchip. The microchip is scanned and a registry quickly identifies you as the owner.

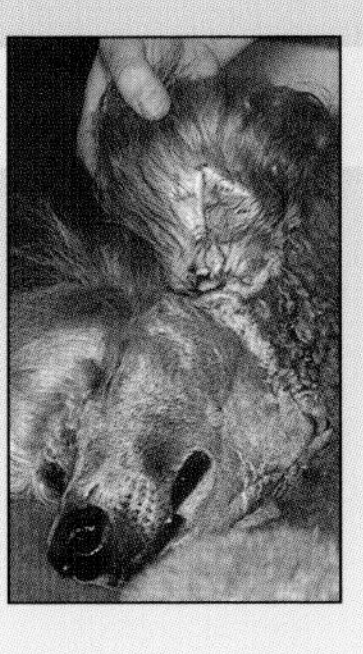

This is not only protection against theft, but should the dog run away or go chasing a squirrel and get lost, you have a fair chance of getting it back.

Tattooing is done on various parts of the dog, from its belly to its cheeks. The number tattooed can be your telephone number or any other number that you can easily memorize. When professional dog thieves see a tattooed dog, they usually lose interest in it. Both microchipping and tattooing can be done at your local veterinary clinic.

TRAINING YOUR POODLE

REAP THE REWARDS

If you start with a normal, healthy dog and give him time, patience and some carefully executed lessons, you will reap the rewards of that training for the life of the dog. And what a

life it will be! The two of you will find immeasurable pleasure in the companionship you have built together with love, respect and understanding.

Poodles have been trained to accomplish thousands of tasks. Few breeds can boast such an expansive repertory of roles—from flawless show dog to circus performer, and just about everything in between! Nonetheless, Poodles are not born with built-in commands. They must be trained just like any other dog, although their propensity for learning is greater than the majority of breeds. They live to please their masters and love to see their masters' delight.

To train your Poodle, you may like to enroll in an obedience class. Teach him good manners as you learn how and why he behaves the way he does. Find out how to communicate with your dog and how to recognize and understand his communications with you. Suddenly the dog takes on a new role in your life—he is clever, interesting, well behaved and fun to be with. He demonstrates his bond of devotion to you daily. In other words, your Poodle does wonders for your ego because he constantly reminds you that you are not only his leader, you are his hero!

Those involved with teaching dog obedience and counseling

owners about their dogs' behavior have discovered some interesting facts about dog ownership. For example, training dogs when they are puppies results in the highest rate of success in developing well-mannered and well-adjusted adult dogs. Training an older dog, from six months to six years of age, can produce almost equal results, providing that the owner accepts the dog's slower rate of learning capability and is willing to work patiently to help the dog succeed at developing to his fullest potential. Unfortunately, many owners of untrained adult dogs lack the patience factor, so they do not persist until their dogs are successful at learning particular behaviors.

Training a puppy aged 10 to 16 weeks (20 weeks at the most) is like working with a dry sponge in a pool of water. The pup soaks up whatever you show him and constantly looks for more things to do and learn. At this early age, his body is not yet producing hormones, and therein lies the reason for such a high rate of success. Without hormones, he is focused on his owners and not particularly interested in investigating other places, dogs, people, etc. You are his leader: his provider of food, water, shelter and security. He latches onto you and wants to stay close. He will usually follow you from room to room, will not let you out of his sight when you are outdoors with him and will respond in like manner to the people and animals you encounter. If you greet a friend warmly, he will be happy to greet

PARENTAL GUIDANCE

Training a dog is a life experience. Many parents admit that much of what they know about raising children they learned from caring for their dogs. Dogs respond to love,

fairness and guidance, just as children do. Become a good dog owner and you may become an even better parent.

THE HAND THAT FEEDS

To a dog's way of thinking, your hands are like his mouth in terms of a defense mechanism. If you squeeze him too tightly, he might just bite you because that would be his normal response. This is not aggressive biting and, although all biting should be discouraged, you need the discipline in learning how to handle your dog.

the person as well. If, however, you are hesitant or anxious about the approach of a stranger, he will respond accordingly.

Once the puppy begins to produce hormones, his natural curiosity emerges and he begins to investigate the world around him. It is at this time when you may notice that the untrained dog begins to wander away from you and even ignore your commands to stay close. When this behavior becomes a problem, the owner has two choices: get rid of the dog or train him. It is strongly urged that you choose the latter option.

There are usually classes within a reasonable distance from the owner's home, but you also can do a lot to train your dog yourself. Sometimes there are classes available but the tuition is too costly. Whatever the circumstances, the solution to training your Poodle without formal lessons lies within the pages of this book.

This chapter is devoted to helping you train your Poodle at home. If the recommended procedures are followed faithfully, you may expect positive results that will prove rewarding to both you and your dog.

Whether your new charge is a puppy or a mature adult, the methods of teaching and the techniques we use in training basic behaviors are the same. After all, no dog, whether puppy or adult, likes harsh or inhumane methods. All creatures, however, respond favorably to gentle motivational methods and sincere praise and encouragement. Now let us get started.

HOUSEBREAKING

You can train a puppy to relieve itself wherever you choose, but this must be somewhere suitable. You should bear in mind from the outset that when your puppy is old enough to go out in public places, any canine deposits must be removed at once. You will always have to carry with you a small plastic bag or "poop-scoop."

Outdoor training includes such surfaces as grass, soil or cement. Indoor training usually means training your dog to newspaper.

When deciding on the surface and location that you will want your Poodle to use, be sure it is going to be permanent. Training your dog to grass and then changing your mind two months later is extremely difficult for both dog and owner.

Next, choose the command you will use each and every time you want your puppy to void. "Be quick," "Hurry up" and "Let's go" are examples of commands commonly used by dog owners.

Get in the habit of giving the puppy your chosen relief command before you take him out. That way, when he becomes an adult, you will be able to determine if he wants to go out when you ask him. A confirmation will be signs of interest, such as wagging his tail, watching you intently, going to the door, etc.

OPEN MINDS

Dogs are as different from each other as people are. What works for one dog may not work for another. Have an open mind and be patient. If one method of training is unsuccessful, try another until you find what works.

Puppy's Needs

The puppy needs to relieve himself after play periods, after each meal, after he has been sleeping and any time he indicates that he is looking for a place to urinate or defecate.

The urinary and intestinal tract muscles of very young

Poodles are easily housebroken. Choose an out-of-the-way spot in the yard and train your Poodle to his designated relief area.

puppies are not fully developed. Therefore, like human babies, puppies need to relieve themselves frequently.

Take your puppy out often—every hour for an eight-week-old, for example, and always immediately after sleeping and eating. The older the puppy, the less often he will need to relieve himself. Finally, as a mature healthy adult, he will require only three to five relief trips per day.

HOW MANY TIMES A DAY?

AGE	RELIEF TRIPS
To 14 weeks	10
14–22 weeks	8
22–32 weeks	6
Adulthood (dog stops growing)	4

These are estimates, of course, but they are a guide to the minimum number of opportunities a dog should have each day to relieve itself.

Housing

Since the types of housing and control you provide for your puppy have a direct relationship on the success of housebreaking, we consider the various aspects of both before we begin training.

Bringing a new puppy home and turning him loose in your house can be compared to turning a child loose in a sports arena and telling the child that the place is all his! The sheer enormity of the place would be too much for him to handle.

Instead, offer the puppy clearly defined areas where he can play, sleep, eat and live. A room of the house where the family gathers is the most obvious choice. Puppies are social animals and need to feel a part of the pack right from the start. Hearing your voice, watching you while you are doing things and smelling you nearby are all positive reinforcers that he is now a member of your pack. Usually a family room, the kitchen or a nearby adjoining breakfast area is ideal for providing safety and security for both puppy and owner.

Within that room, there should be a smaller area that the puppy can call his own. An alcove, a wire or fiberglass dog crate or a fenced (not boarded!) corner from which he can view the activities of his new family will be fine. The size of the area or crate is the key factor here. The

Accustom the Poodle to his crate at an early age. When he's grown, he will welcome his crate as a child does his own room.

area must be large enough for the puppy to lie down and stretch out as well as stand up without rubbing his head on the top, yet small enough so that he cannot relieve himself at one end and sleep at the other without coming into contact with his droppings before he is fully housebroken.

Dogs are, by nature, clean animals and will not remain close to their relief areas unless forced to do so. In those cases, they then become dirty dogs and usually remain that way for life.

The designated area should be lined with clean bedding and the dog should be offered a toy. Water must always be available, in a non-spill container, once house-breaking has been acheived reliably.

Control

By control, we mean helping the puppy to create a lifestyle pattern that will be compatible to that of his human pack *(you!)*. Just as we guide little children to learn our way of life, we must show the puppy when it is time to play, eat, sleep, exercise and even entertain himself.

Your puppy should always sleep in his crate. He should also learn that, during times of household confusion and excessive human activity, such as at breakfast when family members

TRAINING RULES

If you want to be successful in training your dog, you have four rules to obey yourself:

1. Develop an understanding of how a dog thinks.

2. Do not blame the dog for lack of communication.
3. Define your dog's personality and act accordingly.
4. Have patience and be consistent.

CANINE DEVELOPMENT SCHEDULE

It is important to understand how and at what age a puppy develops into adulthood. If you are a puppy owner, consult the following Canine Development Schedule to determine the stage of development your puppy is currently experiencing. This knowledge will help you as you work with the puppy in the weeks and months ahead.

Period	Age	Characteristics
First to Third	Birth to Seven Weeks	Puppy needs food, sleep and warmth, and responds to simple and gentle touching. Needs mother for security and disciplining. Needs littermates for learning and interacting with other dogs. Pup learns to function within a pack and learns pack order of dominance. Begin socializing pup with adults and children for short periods. Pup begins to become aware of his environment.
Fourth	Eight to Twelve Weeks	Brain is fully developed. Needs socializing with outside world. Remove from mother and littermates. Needs to change from canine pack to human pack. Human dominance necessary. Fear period occurs between 8 and 12 weeks. Avoid fright and pain.
Fifth	Thirteen to Sixteen Weeks	Training and formal obedience should begin. Less association with other dogs, more with people, places, situations. Period will pass easily if you remember this is pup's change-to-adolescence time. Be firm and fair. Flight instinct prominent. Permissiveness and over-disciplining can do permanent damage. Praise for good behavior.
Juvenile	Four to Eight Months	Another fear period about 7 to 8 months of age. It passes quickly, but be cautious of fright and pain. Sexual maturity reached. Dominant traits established. Dog should understand sit, down, come and stay by now.

Note: These are approximate time frames. Allow for individual differences in puppies.

are preparing for the day, he can play by himself in safety and comfort in his designated area. Each time you leave the puppy alone, he should understand exactly where he is to stay. Puppies are chewers. They cannot tell the difference between lamp cords, television wires, shoes,

TEACHING MANNERS

Dogs will do anything for your attention. If you reward the dog when he is calm and attentive, you will develop a well-mannered dog. If, on the other hand, you greet your

dog excitedly and encourage him to wrestle and roughhouse with you, the dog will greet you the same way and you will have a hyper dog on your hands.

Poodles excel in many areas of obedience work, from the basic commands to advanced agility and obedience trials.

table legs, etc.Chewing into a television wire, for example, can be fatal to the puppy, while a shorted wire can start a fire in the house.

If the puppy chews on the arm of the chair when he is alone, you would probably discipline him angrily when you get home. Thus, he makes the association that your coming home means he is going to be punished. (He will not remember chewing the chair and is incapable of making the association of the discipline with his naughty deed.)

Other times of excitement, such as family parties, visits from friends, etc., can be fun for the puppy, provided he can view the activities from the security of his designated area. He is not underfoot and he is not being fed all sorts of tidbits that will probably cause him stomach distress, yet he still feels a part of the fun.

Schedule

A puppy should be taken to his relief area each time he is released from his designated area, after meals, after a play session, when he first awakens in the morning (at age eight weeks, this can mean 5 a.m.!). The puppy will indicate that he's ready "to go" by circling or sniffing busily—do not misinterpret these signs. For a puppy less than ten weeks of age, a routine of taking him out every hour is necessary. As the puppy grows, he will be able to wait for

THE SUCCESS METHOD

Success that comes by luck is usually short-lived. Success that comes by well-thought-out proven methods is often more easily achieved and permanent. This is the Success Method. It is designed to give you, the puppy owner, a simple yet proven way to help your puppy develop clean living habits and a feeling of security in his new environment.

6 Steps to Successful Crate Training

1 Tell the puppy "Crate time!" and place him in the crate with a small treat (a piece of cheese or half of a biscuit). Let him stay in the crate for five minutes while you are in the same room. Then release him and praise lavishly. Never release him when he is fussing. Wait until he is quiet before you let him out.

2 Repeat Step 1 several times a day.

3 The next day, place the puppy in the crate as before. Let him stay there for ten minutes. Do this several times.

4 Continue building time in five-minute increments until the puppy stays in his crate for 30 minutes with you in the room. Always take him to his relief area after prolonged periods in his crate.

5 Now go back to Step 1 and let the puppy stay in his crate for five minutes, this time while you are out of the room.

6 Once again, build crate time in five-minute increments with you out of the room. When the puppy will stay willingly in his crate (he may even fall asleep!) for 30 minutes with you out of the room, he will be ready to stay in it for several hours at a time.

longer periods of time.

Keep trips to his relief area short. Stay no more than five or six minutes and then return to the house. If he goes during that time, praise him lavishly and take him indoors immediately. If he does not, but he has an accident when you go back indoors, pick him up immediately, say "No! No!" and return to his relief area. Wait a few minutes, then return to the house again. Never hit a puppy or rub his face in urine or excrement when he has an accident!

Always clean up after your dog, whether you're in a public place or your own garden.

Once indoors, put the puppy in his crate until you have had time to clean up his accident. Then release him to the family area and watch him more closely than before. Chances are, his accident was a result of your not picking up his signal or waiting too long before offering him the opportunity to relieve himself. Never hold a grudge against the puppy for accidents.

Let the puppy learn that going outdoors means it is time to relieve himself, not to play. Once trained, he will be able to play indoors and out and still differentiate between the times for play versus the times for relief.

Help him develop regular hours for naps, being alone, playing by himself and just resting, all in his crate. Encourage him to entertain himself while you are busy with your activities. Let him learn that having you

SPEAKING "DOG"

Dogs do not understand our language. They can be trained to react to a certain sound, at a certain volume. If you say "No, Oliver" in a very soft, pleasant voice, it will not have the same meaning as "No, Oliver!!" when you raise your voice. Dogs must rely on tone of voice as much as the word or command that you use. You should never use the dog's name during a reprimand, just the command No!! You never want the dog to associate his name (which you use to call him) with a negative command.

If your home is drafty, consider purchasing a crate cover to keep your Poodle warm while he's resting.

near is comforting, but it is not your main purpose in life to provide him with your undivided attention.

Each time you put a puppy in his own area, use the same command, whatever suits best. Soon, he will run to his crate or special area when he hears you say those words.

Your Poodle will look to you for equitable treatment and guidance. Be fair and positive and you will see results almost instantly.

Remember that one of the primary ingredients in housebreaking your puppy is control. Regardless of your lifestyle, there will always be occasions when you will need to have a place where your dog can stay and be safe. Crate training is the answer for now and in the future.

In conclusion, a few key elements are really all you need for a successful housebreaking method—consistency, frequency, praise, control and supervision. By following these procedures with a normal, healthy puppy, you and the puppy will soon be past the stage of "accidents" and ready to move on to a clean and rewarding life together.

ROLES OF DISCIPLINE, REWARD AND PUNISHMENT

Discipline, training one to act in accordance with rules, brings order to life. It is as simple as that. Without discipline, particularly in a group society, chaos reigns supreme and the group will eventually perish. Humans and canines are social animals and need some form of discipline in order to function effectively. They must procure food, protect their home base

and their young and reproduce to keep the species going.

If there were no discipline in the lives of social animals, they would eventually die from starvation and/or predation by other stronger animals.

In the case of domestic canines, dogs need discipline in their lives in order to understand how their pack (you and other family members) functions and how they must act in order to survive.

A large humane society in a highly populated area recently surveyed dog owners regarding their satisfaction with their relationships with their dogs. People who had trained their dogs were 75% more satisfied with their pets than those who had never trained their dogs.

Dr. Edward Thorndike, a psychologist, established *Thorndike's Theory of Learning*, which states that a behavior that results in a pleasant event tends to be repeated. A behavior that results in an unpleasant event tends not to be repeated. It is this theory on which training methods are based today. For example, if you manipulate a dog to perform a specific behavior and reward him for doing it, he is likely to do it again because he enjoyed the end result.

Occasionally, punishment, a penalty inflicted for an offense, is necessary. The best type of punishment often comes from an outside source. For example, a child is told not to touch the

THINK BEFORE YOU BARK!

Dogs are sensitive to their master's moods and emotions. Use your voice wisely when communicating with your dog. Never raise your voice at your dog unless

you are trying to correct him. Speak in a clear authoritative voice so that your dog recognizes that you are giving a command. It is your responsibility to make your dog understand your language. "Barking" at your dog can become as meaningless as "dogspeak" is to you.

The training collar and leash must be easy to put on and take off your Poodle.

stove because he may get burned. He disobeys and touches the stove. In doing so, he receives a burn. From that time on, he respects the heat of the stove and avoids contact with it. Therefore, a behavior that results in an unpleasant event tends not to be repeated.

A good example of a dog's learning the hard way is the dog who chases the house cat. He is told many times to leave the cat alone, yet he persists in teasing the cat. Then, one day he begins

Use treats judiciously when training your Poodle. Most Poodles love tasty treats and will do anything for them... including misbehave!

FETCH!

Play fetching games with your puppy in an enclosed area where he can retrieve his toy and bring it back to you. Always use a toy or object designated just for this purpose. Never use a shoe, sock or other item he may later confuse with those in your closet or underneath your chair.

chasing the cat, but the cat turns and swipes a claw across the dog's face, leaving him with a painful gash on his nose. The final result is that the dog stops chasing the cat.

TRAINING EQUIPMENT

Collar and Leash

For a Poodle, the collar and leash that you use for training must be one with which you are easily able to work, not too heavy for the dog and perfectly safe.

Treats

Have a bag of treats on hand. Something nutritious and easy to swallow works best. Use a soft treat, a chunk of cheese or a piece of cooked chicken rather than a dry biscuit. By the time the dog has finished chewing a dry treat, he will forget why he is being rewarded in the first place! Using food rewards will not teach a dog to beg at the table—the only way to teach a dog to beg at the table is to give him food from the table. In training, rewarding the dog with a food treat will help him associate praise and the treats with learning new behaviors that obviously please his owner.

TRAINING BEGINS: ASK THE DOG A QUESTION

In order to teach your dog anything, you must first get his attention. After all, he cannot learn anything if he is looking away from you with his mind on something else.

To get your Poodle's attention, ask him "School?" and immediately walk over to him and give him a treat as you tell him "Good dog." Wait a minute or two and repeat the routine, this time with a treat in your hand as you approach within a foot of the dog. Do not go directly

Alertness and intelligence are traits evident in the Poodle's expression, assuring that you'll have an attentive student.

to him, but stop about a foot short of him and hold out the treat as you ask, "School?" He will see you approaching with a treat in your hand and most likely begin walking toward you. As you meet, give him the treat and praise again.

The third time, ask the question, have a treat in your hand and walk only a short distance toward the dog so that he must walk almost all the way to you. As he reaches you, give him the treat and praise again.

THE GOLDEN RULE

The golden rule of dog training is simple. For each question (command), there is only one correct answer (reaction). One command = one reaction. This rule applies to all

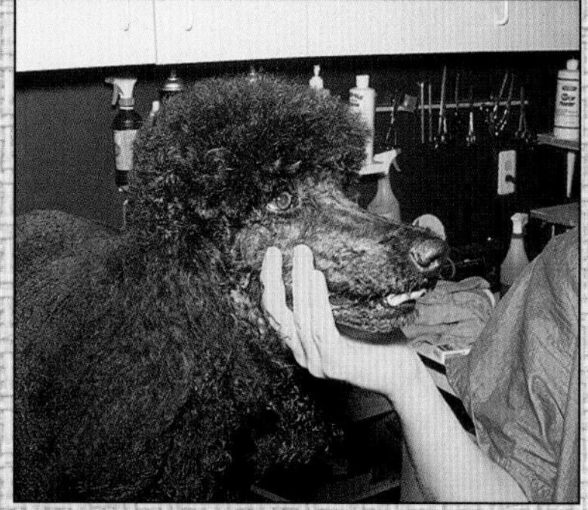

that you do with your Poodle: teaching the house rules, practicing obedience commands, training to behave during grooming, etc.

By this time, the dog will probably be getting the idea that if he pays attention to you, especially when you ask that question, it will pay off in treats and enjoyable activities for him. In other words, he learns that "school" means spending time with you that results in treats and positive attention for him.

Remember that the dog does not understand your verbal language, he only recognizes sounds. Your question translates to a series of sounds for him, and those sounds become the signal to go to you and pay attention; if he does, he will get to interact with you plus receive treats and praise.

THE BASIC COMMANDS

Teaching Sit

Now that you have the dog's attention, attach his leash and hold it in your left hand and a food treat in your right. Place your food hand at the dog's nose and let him lick the treat but not take it from you. Say "Sit" and slowly raise your food hand from in front of the dog's nose up over his head so that he is looking at the ceiling. As he bends his head upward, he will have to bend his knees to maintain his balance. As he bends his knees, he will assume a sit position. At that point, release the food treat and praise lavishly with comments such as "Good dog! Good sit!", etc. Remember to always praise enthusiastically, because dogs relish verbal praise from their owners and feel so proud of themselves whenever they accomplish a behavior.

You will not use food forever in getting the dog to obey your commands. Food is only used to teach new behaviors, and once the dog knows what you want when you give a specific command, you will wean him off the food treats but still maintain the verbal praise. After all, you will always have your voice with you, and there will be many times when you have no food rewards but expect the dog to obey.

If the Poodle does not respond to the treat while learning the sit command, you may need to assist him a little by pushing gently on his hindquarters.

DOUBLE JEOPARDY

A dog in jeopardy never lies down. He stays alert on his feet because instinct tells him that he may have to run away or fight for his survival. Therefore, if a dog feels threatened

or anxious, he will not lie down. Consequently, it is important to have the dog calm and relaxed as he learns the down exercise.

The proper sit position. Poodles make excellent and patient students.

Teaching the down position is more difficult than teaching the sit, but it can be accomplished with practice and consistency.

Teaching Down

Teaching the down exercise is easy when you understand how the dog perceives the down position, and it is very difficult when you do not. Dogs perceive the down position as a submissive one; therefore, teaching the down exercise using a forceful method can sometimes make the dog develop such a fear of the down that he either runs away when you say "Down" or he attempts to snap at the person who tries to force him down.

Have the dog sit close alongside your left leg, facing in the same direction as you are. Hold the leash in your left hand and a food treat in your right. Now place your left hand lightly on the top of the dog's shoulders where they meet above the spinal cord. Do not push down on the dog's shoulders; simply rest your left hand there so you can guide the dog to lie down close to your left leg rather than to swing away from your side when he drops.

Now place the food hand at the dog's nose, say "Down" very softly (almost a whisper) and slowly lower the food hand to the dog's front feet. When the food hand reaches the floor, begin moving it forward along the floor in front of the dog. Keep talking softly to the dog, saying things like, "Do you want this treat? You can do this, good dog." Your reassuring tone of voice will help calm the dog as he tries to follow the food hand in order to get the treat.

When the dog's elbows touch the floor, release the food and praise softly. Try to get the dog to maintain that down position for several seconds before you let him sit up again. The goal here is to get the dog to settle down and not feel threatened in the down position.

KEEP SMILING

Never train your dog, puppy or adult, when you are mad or in a sour mood. Dogs are very sensitive to human feelings, especially anger. If your dog senses that you are angry or upset, he will connect your anger with his training and learn to resent or fear his training sessions.

It is not difficult to teach the stay command once the dog has been taught the sit and down positions.

OBEDIENCE PRACTICE

Occasionally, a dog and owner who have not attended formal classes have been able to earn entry-level titles by obtaining competition rules and regulations from a local kennel club and practicing on their own to a degree of perfection. Obtaining the higher level titles, however, almost always requires extensive training under the tutelage of experienced instructors. In addition, the more difficult levels require more specialized equipment whereas the beginning levels do not.

Teaching Stay

It is easy to teach the dog to stay in either a sit or a down position. Again, we use food and praise during the teaching process as we help the dog to understand exactly what it is that we are expecting him to do.

To teach the sit/stay, start with the dog sitting on your left side as before and hold the leash in your left hand. Have a food treat in your right hand and place your food hand at the dog's nose. Say "Stay" and step out on your right foot to stand directly in front of the dog, toe to toe, as he licks and nibbles the treat. Be sure to

As you progress with the stay exercise, increase the distance between you and your Poodle.

keep his head facing upward to maintain the sit position. Count to five and then swing around to stand next to the dog again with him on your left. As soon as you get back to the original position, release the food and praise lavishly.

To teach the down/stay, do the down as previously described. As soon as the dog lies down, say "Stay" and step out on your right foot just as you did in the sit/stay. Count to five and then return to stand beside the dog with him on your left side. Release the treat and praise as always.

Within a week or ten days, you can begin to add a bit of distance between you and your dog when you leave him. When you do, use your left hand open with the palm facing the dog as a stay signal, much the same as the hand signal a police officer uses to stop traffic at an intersection. Hold the food treat in your right hand as before, but this time the food is not touching the dog's nose. He will watch the food hand and quickly learn that he is going to get that treat as soon as you return to his side.

When you can stand 3 feet away from your dog for 30 seconds, you can then begin building time and distance in both stays. Eventually, the dog can be expected to remain in the stay position for prolonged periods of time until you return to him or call him to you. Always praise lavishly when he stays.

HONOR AND OBEY

Dogs are the most honorable animals in existence. They consider another species (humans) as their own. They interface with you. You are their leader. Puppies perceive children to be on their level; their actions around small children are different from their behavior around their adult masters.

Teaching Come

If you make teaching "come" an enjoyable experience, you should never have a student that does not love the game or that fails to come when called. The secret, it seems, is never to teach the word "come."

At times when an owner most wants his dog to come when called, the owner is likely upset or anxious, and he allows these feelings to come through in the tone of his voice when he calls his dog. Hearing that desperation in his owner's voice, the dog fears the results of going to him and therefore either disobeys outright or runs in the opposite direction. The secret, therefore, is to teach the dog a game and, when you want him to come to you, simply play the game. It is practically a no-fail solution!

To begin, have several members of your family take a few food treats and each go into a different room in the house. Take turns calling the dog, and each person should celebrate the dog's finding him with a treat and lots of happy praise. When a person calls the dog, he is actually inviting the dog to find him and get a treat as a reward for "winning."

A few turns of the "Where are you?" game and the dog will understand that everyone is playing the game and that each person has a big celebration awaiting his success at locating him or her. Once he learns to love the game, simply calling out "Where are you?" will bring him running from wherever he is when he hears that all-important question.

Every Poodle has individual talents. Catching a large ball in mid-air might be a part of the fetch-and-return game you play with your pet.

The come command is recognized as one of the most important things to teach a dog, but there are trainers who work with thousands of dogs and never teach the actual word "come." Yet these dogs will race to respond to a person who uses the dog's name followed by "Where are you?" For example, a woman has a 12-year-old companion dog who went blind, but who never fails to locate her owner when asked, "Where are you?"

Children particularly love to play this game with their dogs. Children can hide in smaller places like a shower or bathtub, behind a bed or under a table. The dog needs to work a little bit harder to find these hiding places, but, when he does, he loves to celebrate with a treat and hug from a favorite youngster.

SAFETY FIRST

Your dog's first concern is safety. The dogs we keep today have the same pack instinct as their ancestors. Because of this pack instinct, your dog wants to know that he and his pack

are not in danger, and that his pack has a strong, capable leader. You must establish yourself as the leader early on so that your dog will trust that you will take care of him and the pack.

TEACHING HEEL

Heeling means that the dog walks beside the owner without pulling. It takes time and patience on the owner's part to succeed at teaching the dog that he (the owner) will not proceed unless the dog is walking calmly beside him. Pulling out ahead on the leash is definitely not acceptable.

Begin with holding the leash in your left hand as the dog sits beside your left leg. Move the loop end of the leash to your right hand but keep your left hand short on the leash so it keeps the dog in close next to you.

Say "Heel" and step forward on your left foot. Keep the dog close to you and take three steps. Stop and have the dog sit next to you in what we now call the heel position. Praise verbally, but do not touch the dog. Hesitate a moment and begin again with "Heel," taking three steps and stopping, at which point the dog is told to sit again.

You can proudly and comfortably walk with your Poodle if he is trained to heel.

Your goal here is to have the dog walk those three steps without pulling on the leash. When he will walk calmly beside you for three steps without pulling, increase the number of steps you take to five. When he will walk politely beside you while you take five steps, you can increase the length of your walk to ten steps. Keep increasing the length of your stroll until the dog will walk quietly beside you without pulling as long as you want him to heel. When you stop heeling, indicate to the dog that the exercise is over by verbally praising as you pet him and say "OK, good dog." The "OK" is used as a release word, meaning that the exercise is finished and the dog is free to relax.

If you are dealing with a dog who insists on pulling you around, simply "put on your brakes" and stand your ground until the dog realizes that the two of you are not going anywhere until he is beside you and moving at your pace, not his. It may take some time just standing there to convince the dog that you are the leader and you will be the one to decide on the direction and speed of your travel.

PLAN TO PLAY

The Poodle should have regular play and exercise sessions when he is with you or a family member. Exercise for a very young puppy can consist of a short walk around the house or yard. Playing can include fetching games. For a puppy,

remember to restrict play periods to indoors within his living area (the family room, for example) until he is completely housebroken. Play breaks are a good way to avoid monotony in training sessions.

PRACTICE MAKES PERFECT

- Have training lessons with your dog every day in several short segments—three to five times a day for a few minutes at a time is ideal.
- Do not have long practice sessions.

The dog will become easily bored.

- Never practice when you are tired, ill, worried or in an otherwise negative mood. This will transmit to the dog and may have an adverse effect on his performance.

Think fun, short and above all POSITIVE! End each session on a high note, rather than a failed exercise, and make sure to give a lot of praise. Enjoy the training and help your dog enjoy it, too.

Each time the dog looks up at you or slows down to give a slack leash between the two of you, quietly praise him and say, "Good heel. Good dog." Eventually, the dog will begin to respond and within a few days he will be walking politely beside you without pulling on the leash. At first, the training sessions should be kept short and very positive; soon the dog will be able to walk nicely with you for increasingly longer distances. Remember also to give the dog free time to run and play when you have finished heel practice.

WEANING OFF FOOD IN TRAINING

Food is used in training new behaviors. Once the dog understands what behavior goes with a specific command, it is time to start weaning him off the food treats. At first, give a treat after each exercise. Then, start to give a treat only after every other exercise. Mix up the times when you offer a food reward and the times when you offer only praise so that the dog will never know when he is going to receive both food and praise and when he is going to receive only praise.

OBEDIENCE CLASSES

It is a good idea to enroll in an obedience class if one is available in your area. If yours is a show dog, showing classes would be more appropriate. Many areas have dog clubs that offer basic obedience training as well as preparatory classes for obedience competition. There are also local dog trainers who offer similar classes.

At obedience trials, dogs can earn titles at various levels of competition. The beginning levels of competition include basic behaviors such as sit, down, heel, etc. The more advanced levels of competition include jumping, retrieving, scent discrimination and signal work. The advanced levels require a dog and owner to put a lot of time and effort into their training, and the titles that can be earned at these levels of competition are very prestigious.

SHOW OFF!

What a sight it is to see a Poodle in the show ring, displaying his graceful gait. Heel training is necessary for all

dogs, and essential for show dogs, as the judge looks for not only correct structure and movement but also polite behavior on-lead.

OTHER ACTIVITIES FOR LIFE

Whether a dog is trained in the structured environment of a class or alone with his owner at home, there are many activities that can bring fun and rewards to both owner and dog once they have mastered basic control.

Teaching the dog to help out around the home, in the yard or on the farm provides great satisfaction to both dog and owner. In addition, the dog's help makes life a little easier for his owner and raises his stature as a valued companion to his family. It helps to give the dog a purpose by occupying his mind and providing an outlet for his energy.

Backpacking is an exciting and healthy activity that the dog can be taught without assistance from more than his owner. The exercise of walking and climbing

Poodles are agile, intelligent and trainable. You can easily take advantage of these characteristics and train your Poodle in obedience competitions.

OBEDIENCE SCHOOL

Taking your dog to an obedience school may be the best investment in time and money you can ever make. You will enjoy the benefits for the lifetime of your dog and you will have the opportunity to meet people with similar expectations for their companion dogs.

is good for man and dog alike, and the bond that they develop together is priceless. The dog should not carry more than one-sixth of his body weight.

If you like to volunteer, consider doing therapy-dog work with your Poodle. The Poodle's intelligence, intuition and love of company make him a delightful and welcome visitor to hospitals and nursing homes.

If you are interested in participating in organized competition with your Poodle, there are activities other than obedience in which you and your dog can become involved. Agility is a popular and enjoyable sport where dogs run through an obstacle course that includes various jumps, tunnels and other exercises to test the dog's speed and coordination. The owners run through the exercise beside their dogs to give commands and to guide them through the course. Although competitive, the focus is on fun—it's fun to do, fun to watch and great exercise. Agility is something to which the intelligent and active Poodle is naturally well suited.

Breed clubs offer many types of events that may be of interest to Poodle owners. Tracking, water tests, flyball and other competitive endeavors allow the Poodle to expend some energy and use his brain. Contact a Poodle club or all-breed club to find out more about events in your area.

A well-trained Poodle is a pleasant and polite companion.

Skeletal Structure of the Poodle

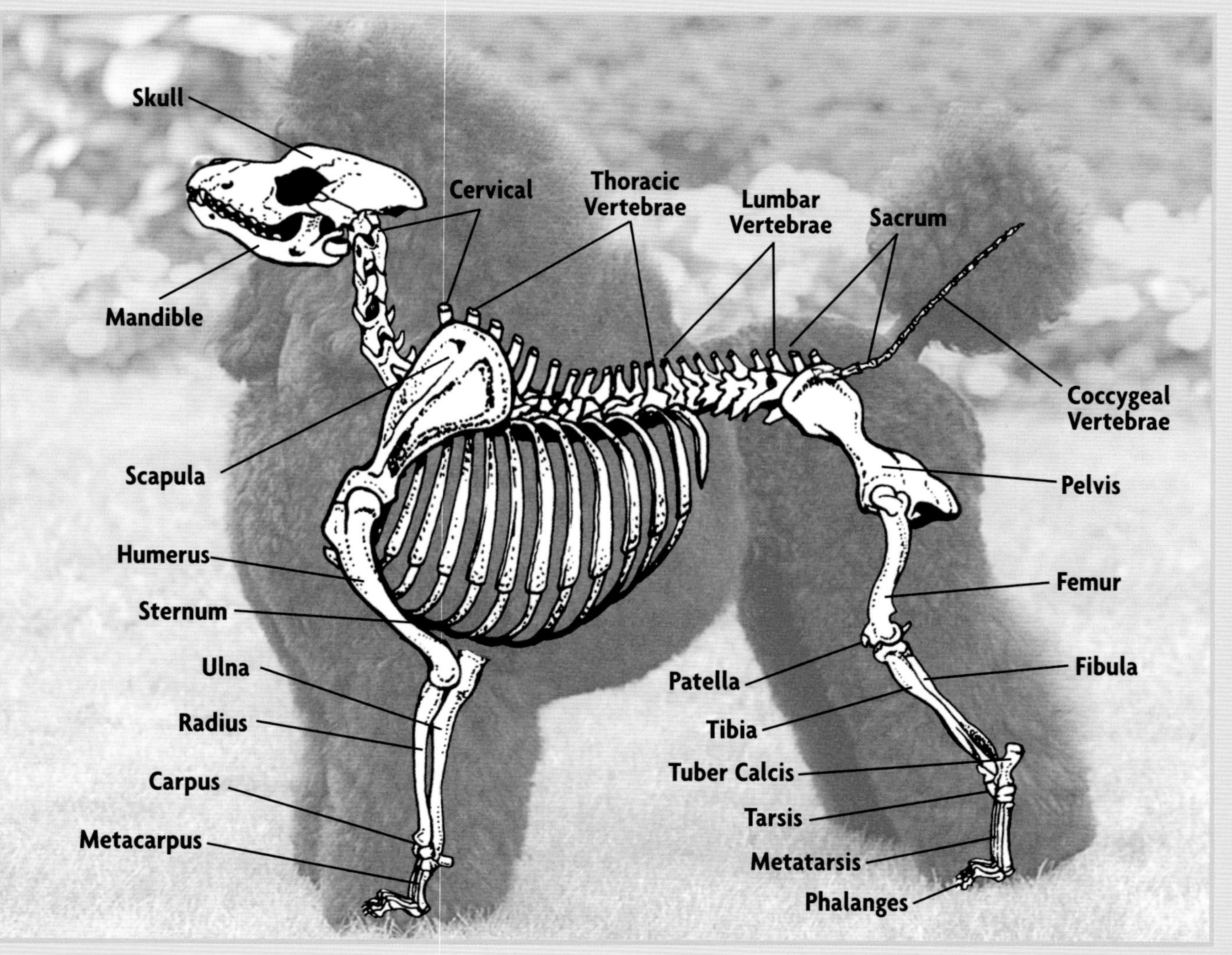

HEALTH CARE OF YOUR

POODLE

Dogs suffer from many of the same physical illnesses as people. They might even share many of the same psychological problems. Since people usually know more about human diseases than canine maladies, many of the terms used in this chapter will be familiar but not necessarily those used by veterinarians. We will use the term *x-ray*, instead of the more acceptable term *radiograph*. We will also use the familiar term *symptoms* even though dogs don't have symptoms, which are verbal descriptions of the patient's feelings: dogs have *clinical signs*. Since dogs can't speak, we have to look for clinical signs...but we still use the term *symptoms* in this book.

As a general rule, medicine is *practiced*. That term is not arbitrary. Medicine is a constantly changing art as we learn more and more about genetics, electronic aids (like CAT scans and MRIs) and daily laboratory advances. There are many dog maladies, like canine hip dysplasia, which are not universally treated in the same manner. Some veterinarians opt for surgery more often than others do.

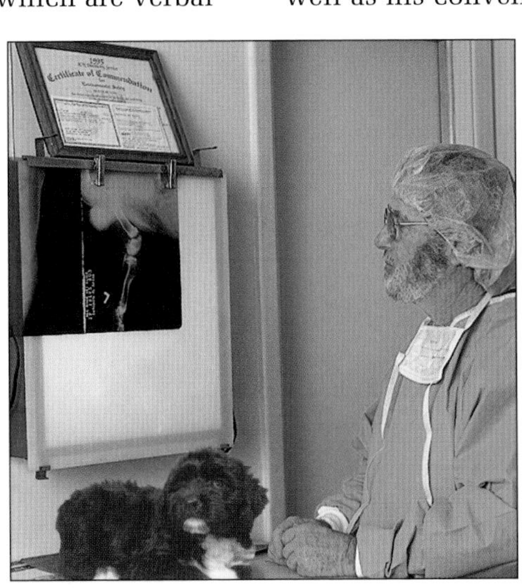

Your chosen veterinarian should be familiar with the latest technologies and have all the necessary equipment at his disposal.

SELECTING A VETERINARIAN

Your selection of a veterinarian should be based upon his skills, reputation and personality, as well as his convenience to your home. You require a veterinarian who is close by because you might have emergencies or need to make multiple visits for treatments. You require a vet who has services that you might require such as tattooing and grooming facilities, as well as sophisticated pet supplies and a good reputation for ability and

A typical vet's income, categorized according to services provided. This survey dealt with small-animal practices.

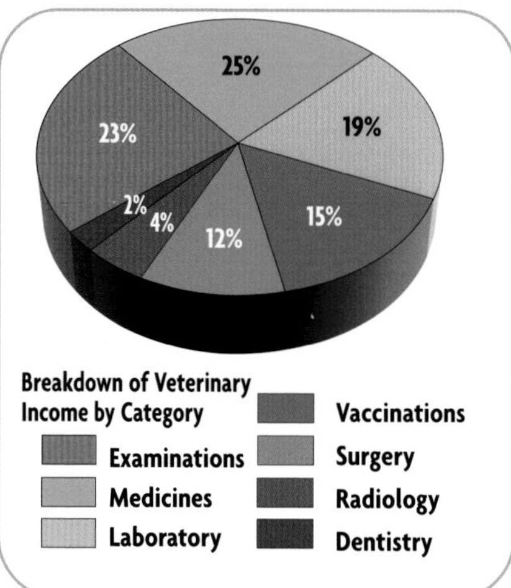

responsiveness. There is nothing more frustrating than having to wait a day or more to get a response from your veterinarian.

All veterinarians are licensed and their diplomas and/or certificates should be displayed in their waiting rooms. There are, however, many veterinary specialties that usually require further studies and internships. There are specialists in heart problems (veterinary cardiologists), skin problems (veterinary dermatologists), teeth and gum problems (veterinary dentists), eye problems (veterinary ophthalmologists) and x-rays (veterinary radiologists), and surgeons who have specialties in bones, muscles or other organs. Most veterinarians do routine surgery such as neutering, stitching up wounds and docking tails for those breeds in which such is required for show purposes.

When the problem affecting your dog is serious, it is not unusual or impudent to get another medical opinion. You might also want to compare costs among several veterinarians. Veterinary procedures are very costly and, as the treatments available improve, they are going to become more expensive. It is quite acceptable to discuss matters of cost with your vet; if there is more than one treatment option, cost may be a factor in deciding which route to take.

NEUTER/SPAY

Male dogs are neutered. The operation removes the testicles and requires that the dog be

anesthetized. Recovery takes about one week. Females are spayed. This is major surgery and it usually takes a bitch two weeks to recover.

First Aid at a Glance

Burns
Place the affected area under cool water; use ice if only a small area is burned.

Bee/Insect bites
Apply ice to relieve swelling; antihistamine dosed properly.

Animal bites
Clean any bleeding area; apply pressure until bleeding subsides; go to the vet.

Spider bites
Use cold compress and a pressurized pack to inhibit venom's spreading.

Antifreeze poisoning
Immediately induce vomiting by using hydrogen peroxide.

Fish hooks
Removal best handled by vet; hook must be cut in order to remove.

Snake bites
Pack ice around bite; contact vet quickly; identify snake for proper antivenin.

Car accident
Move dog from roadway with blanket; seek veterinary aid.

Shock
Calm the dog, keep him warm; seek immediate veterinary help.

Nosebleed
Apply cold compress to the nose; apply pressure to any visible abrasion.

Bleeding
Apply pressure above the area; treat wound by applying a cotton pack.

Heat stroke
Submerge dog in cold bath; cool down with fresh air and water; go to the vet.

Frostbite/Hypothermia
Warm the dog with a warm bath, electric blankets or hot water bottles.

Abrasions
Clean the wound and wash out thoroughly with fresh water; apply antiseptic.

Remember: an injured dog may attempt to bite a helping hand from fear and confusion. Always muzzle the dog before trying to offer assistance.

PREVENTATIVE MEDICINE

It is much easier, less costly and more effective to practice preventative medicine than to fight bouts of illness and disease. Properly bred puppies come from parents that were selected based upon their genetic disease profiles. Their mother should have been vaccinated, free of all internal and external parasites and properly nourished. For these reasons, a visit to the veterinarian who cared for the dam (mother) is recommended. The dam can pass on disease resistance to her puppies, which can last for eight to ten weeks. She can also pass on parasites and many infections.

A conscientious breeder only breeds animals that have been screened for genetic diseases. This lovely dam is rightly proud of her healthy and attractive litter.

EAR CARE

Not every dog's ears are the same. Ears that are open to the air are healthier than ears with poor air

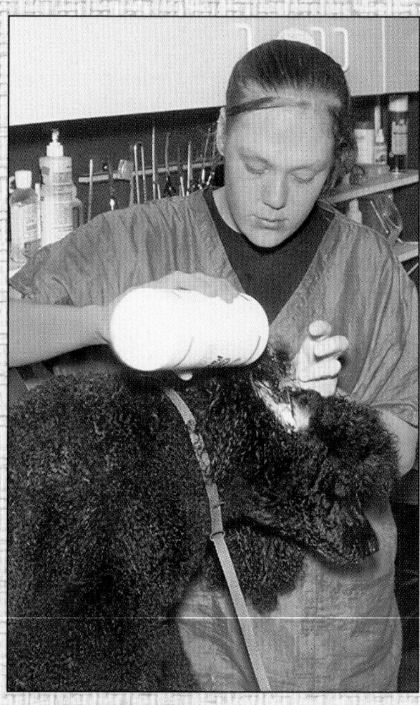

circulation. Sometimes a dog can have two differently shaped ears. You should not probe inside your dog's ears. Only clean that which is accessible with a soft cotton wipe.

That's why it is helpful to learn about the dam's health background.

WEANING TO FIVE MONTHS OLD

Puppies should be weaned by the time they are about two months old. A puppy that remains for at

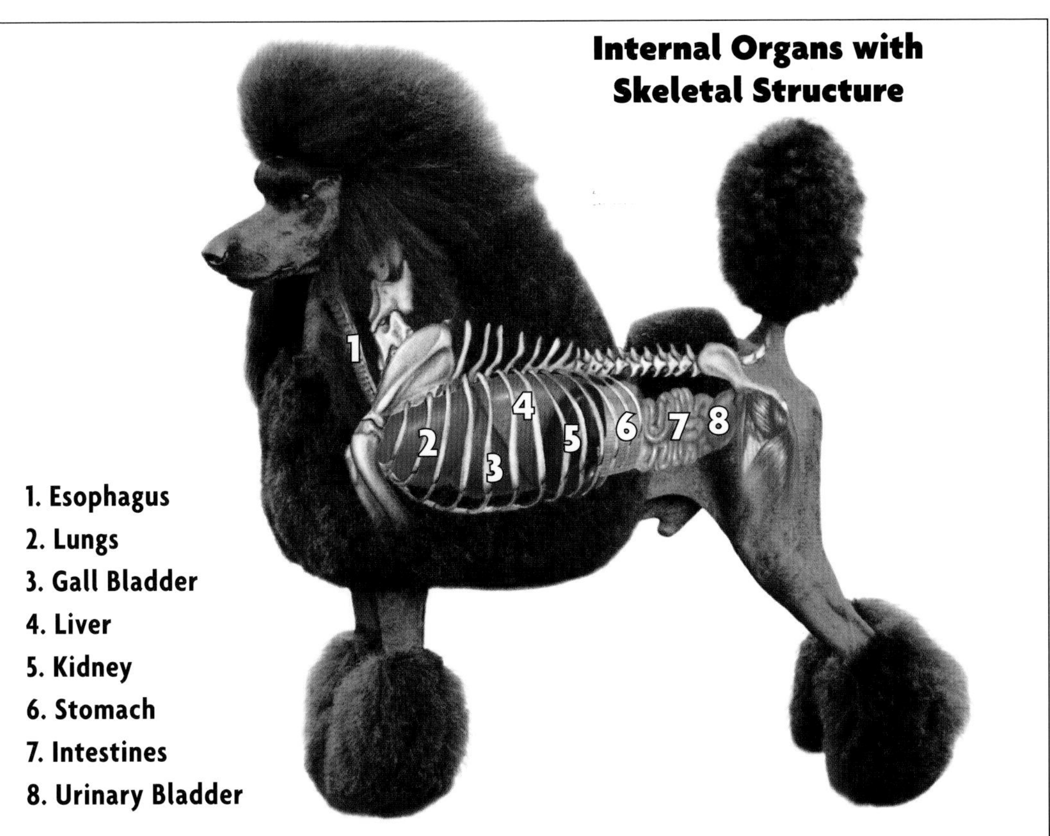

least eight weeks with its mother and littermates usually adapts better to other dogs and people later in its life.

CUSHING'S DISEASE

Cases of hyperactive adrenal glands (Cushing's disease) have been traced to the drinking of highly chlorinated water. Aerate or age your dog's drinking water before offering it.

Some new owners have their puppy examined by a veterinarian immediately, which is a good idea unless the puppy is overtired from the trip home. Vaccination programs usually begin when the puppy is very young.

The puppy will have its teeth examined and have its skeletal conformation and general health checked prior to certification by the veterinarian. Puppies in certain breeds have problems with

HEALTH AND VACCINATION SCHEDULE

AGE IN WEEKS:	3RD	6TH	8TH	10TH	12TH	14TH	16TH	20-24TH
Worm Control	✔	✔	✔	✔	✔	✔	✔	✔
Neutering								✔
Heartworm		✔						✔
Parvovirus		✔		✔		✔		✔
Distemper			✔		✔		✔	
Hepatitis			✔		✔		✔	
Leptospirosis		✔		✔		✔		
Parainfluenza		✔		✔		✔		
Dental Examination			✔					✔
Complete Physical			✔					✔
Temperament Testing			✔					
Coronavirus					✔			
Canine Cough		✔						
Hip Dysplasia							✔	
Rabies								✔

Vaccinations are not instantly effective. It takes about two weeks for the dog's immune system to develop antibodies. Most vaccinations require annual booster shots. Your veterinarian should guide you in this regard.

TEMPERATURE

A dog's normal temperature is 101.5°F, with 100.0°-102.5° considered normal, as each dog's body sets its own

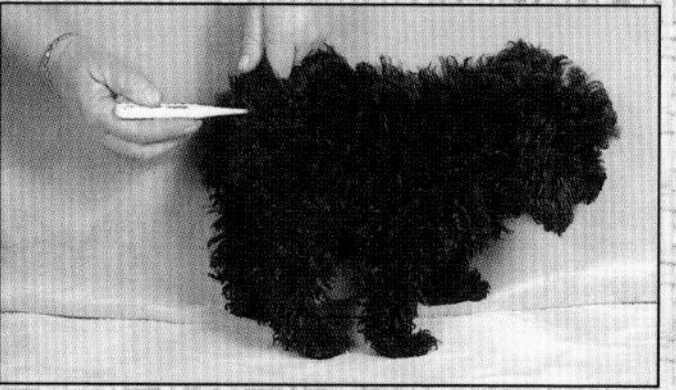

temperature. Take your dog's temperature when you know he is healthy and record it, so that you will have a normal figure to compare when you think he's not feeling well.

their kneecaps, cataracts and other eye problems, heart murmurs and undescended testicles. They may also have personality problems and your veterinarian might have training in temperament testing.

VACCINATION SCHEDULING

Most vaccinations are given by injection and should only be done by a veterinarian. Both he and you should keep a record of the date of the injection, the identification of the vaccine and the amount given. Some vets give a first vaccination at eight weeks, but most dog breeders prefer the course not to commence until about ten weeks

VACCINE ALLERGIES

Vaccines do not work all the time. Sometimes dogs are allergic to the vaccines and many times the antibodies, which are supposed to be stimulated by the vaccines, just are not produced. You should keep your dog in the veterinary clinic for an hour after being vaccinated to be sure there are no allergic or otherwise adverse reactions.

because of the risk of negating any antibodies passed on by the dam. The vaccination scheduling is usually based on a 15-day cycle. You must take your vet's advice as to when to vaccinate, as this may differ according to the vaccine used.

Most vaccinations immunize your puppy against viruses. The usual vaccines contain immunizing doses of several different viruses such as distemper, parvovirus, parainfluenza and hepatitis. There are other vaccines available when

DISEASE REFERENCE CHART

	What is it?	What causes it?	Symptoms
Leptospirosis	Severe disease that affects the internal organs; can be spread to people.	A bacterium, which is often carried by rodents, that enters through mucous membranes and spreads quickly throughout the body.	Range from fever, vomiting and loss of appetite in less severe cases to shock, irreversible kidney damage and possibly death in most severe cases.
Rabies	Potentially deadly virus that infects warm-blooded mammals.	Bite from a carrier of the virus, mainly wild animals.	1st stage: dog exhibits change in behavior, fear. 2nd stage: dog's behavior becomes more aggressive. 3rd stage: loss of coordination, trouble with bodily functions.
Parvovirus	Highly contagious virus, potentially deadly.	Ingestion of the virus, which is usually spread through the feces of infected dogs.	Most common: severe diarrhea. Also vomiting, fatigue, lack of appetite.
Kennel cough	Contagious respiratory infection.	Combination of types of bacteria and virus. Most common: *Bordetella bronchiseptica* bacteria and parainfluenza virus.	Chronic cough.
Distemper	Disease primarily affecting respiratory and nervous system.	Virus that is related to the human measles virus.	Mild symptoms such as fever, lack of appetite and mucous secretion progress to evidence of brain damage, "hard pad."
Hepatitis	Virus primarily affecting the liver.	Canine adenovirus type I (CAV-1). Enters system when dog inhales particles.	Lesser symptoms include listlessness, diarrhea, vomiting. More severe symptoms include "blue-eye" (clumps of virus in eye).
Coronavirus	Virus resulting in digestive problems.	Virus is spread through infected dog's feces.	Stomach upset evidenced by lack of appetite, vomiting, diarrhea.

You should visit your veterinarian immediately upon acquiring your Poodle puppy, and you should continue with the same vet (when possible) for the rest of the dog's life.

the puppy is at risk. You should rely upon professional advice. This is especially true for the booster-shot program. Most vaccination programs require a booster when the puppy is a year old and once a year thereafter. In some cases, circumstances may require more or less frequent immunizations. Canine cough, more formally known as tracheobronchitis, is

treated with a vaccine that is sprayed into the dog's nostrils. Canine cough is usually included in routine vaccination, but this is often not as effective as vaccines for other major diseases.

CORRECTING DYSPLASIA

Any dog can be born with dysplastic problems. Your vet can usually diagnose the potential or actual problem using x-rays. If caught early enough, dysplasia can be corrected.

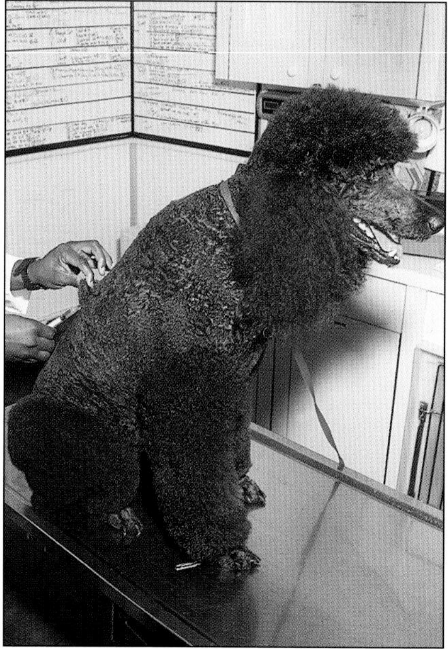

Discuss a vaccination program with your vet. Your vet can advise you of the safest course to follow for your Poodle's inoculations.

Five Months to One Year of Age

Unless you intend to breed or show your dog, neutering the puppy at six months of age is recommended. Discuss this with your veterinarian; most professionals advise neutering the puppy. Neutering (for males) and spaying (for females) have proven to be extremely beneficial. Besides eliminating the possibility of pregnancy, it inhibits (but does not prevent) breast cancer in bitches and prostate cancer in male dogs. Under no circumstances should a bitch be spayed prior to her first season.

Your veterinarian should provide your puppy with a thorough dental evaluation at six months of age, ascertaining whether all of the permanent teeth have erupted properly. A home dental-care regimen should be initiated at six months, including brushing weekly and providing good dental devices (such as nylon bones). Regular dental care promotes healthy teeth, fresh breath and a longer life.

Over One Year of Age

Once a year, your grown dog should visit the vet for an examination and vaccination boosters. Some vets recommend blood tests, a thyroid level check and a dental evaluation to accompany these annual visits. A thorough clinical evaluation by the vet can provide critical background information for your dog. Blood tests are often performed at one year of age, and dental examinations around the third or fourth birthday. In the long run, quality preventative care for your pet can save money, teeth and lives.

DENTAL CARE

A dental examination is in order when the dog is between six months and one year of age so that any

permanent teeth that have erupted incorrectly can be corrected. It is important to begin a brushing routine at home, using a toothbrush made for dogs and specially formulated canine toothpaste. Durable nylon and safe edible chews should be a part of your puppy's arsenal for good health, good teeth and pleasant breath. The vast majority of dogs three to four years old and older has diseases of the gums from lack of dental attention. Using the various types of dental chews can be very effective in controlling dental plaque.

SKIN PROBLEMS IN POODLES

Veterinarians are consulted by dog owners for skin problems more than for any other group of diseases or maladies. Dogs' skin is almost as sensitive as human skin and both can suffer from almost the same ailments (though the occurrence of acne in most breeds of dog is rare!). For this reason, veterinary dermatology has developed into a specialty practiced by many veterinarians.

Since many skin problems have visual symptoms that are almost identical, it requires the skill of an experienced veterinary dermatologist to identify and cure many of the more severe skin disorders. Pet shops sell many treatments for skin problems, but most of the treatments are directed at the symptoms and not the underlying problem(s). If your dog

Left: This remarkable and unique photo shows a dirty, oily Poodle hair magnified 300 times normal size. Right: Magnification of a dirty, oily Poodle hair at 600 times its normal size.

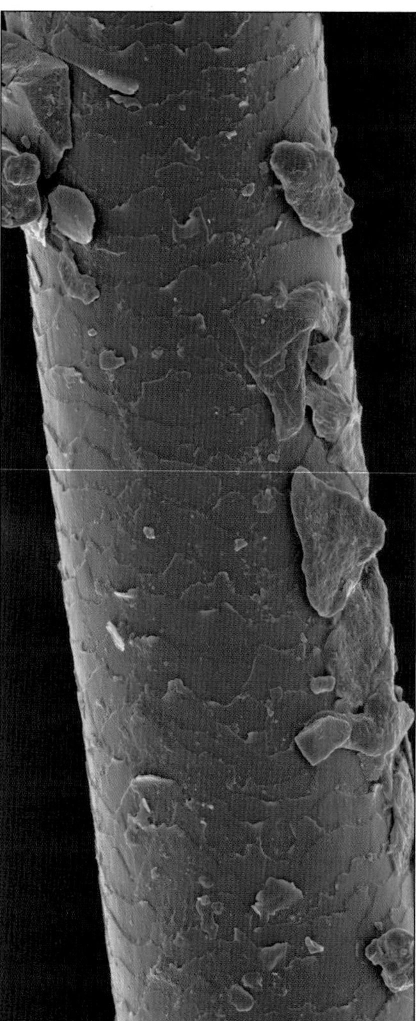

S.E.M. by Dr Dennis Kunkel, University of Hawaii.

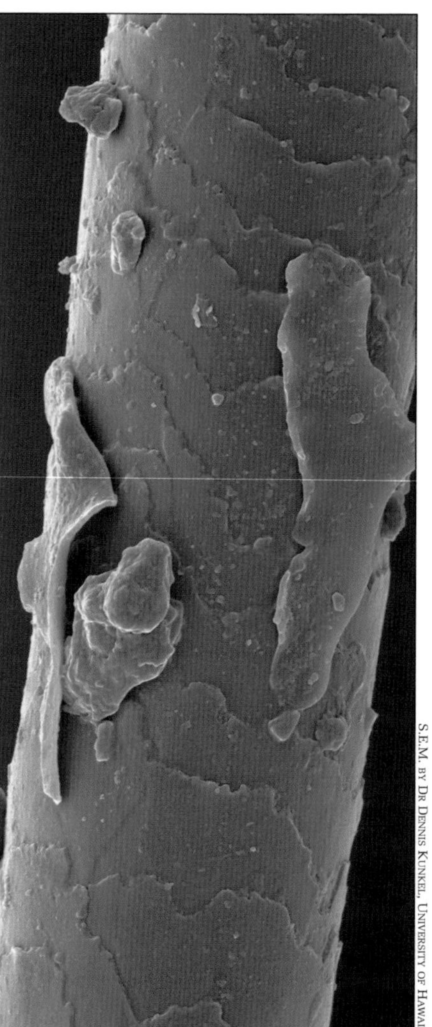

S.E.M. by Dr Dennis Kunkel, University of Hawaii.

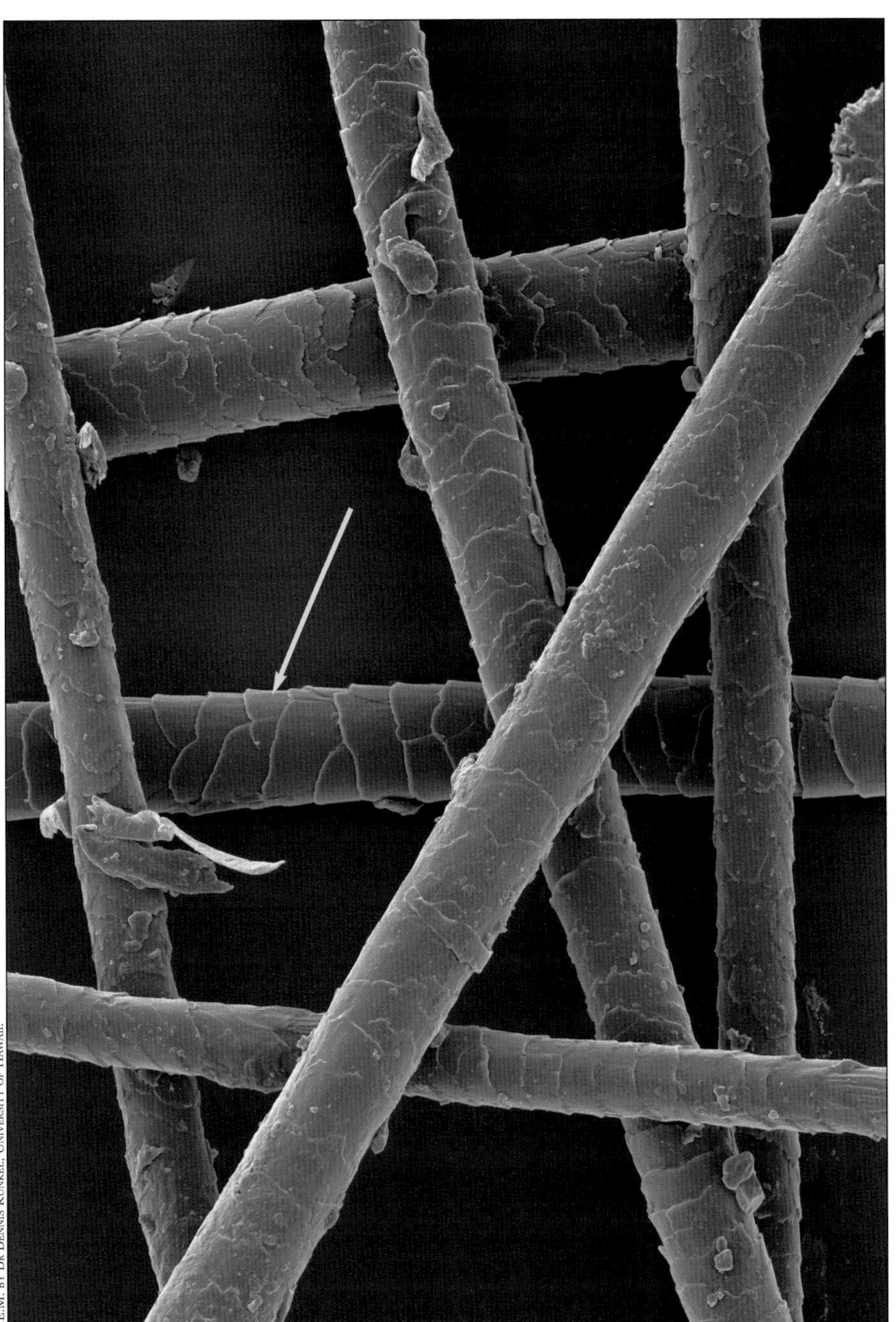

These Poodle hairs are enlarged 250 times their normal size. There is one clean hair; the others are dirty and oily. The clean hair is indicated by the arrow; notice that the cuticle (covering) is uniform and well defined.

S.E.M. BY DR DENNIS KUNKEL, UNIVERSITY OF HAWAII.

CHEMICAL CAUTION

Dogs who have been exposed to lawns sprayed with herbicides have double and triple the rate of

malignant lymphoma. Town dogs are especially at risk, as they are exposed to tailored lawns and yards. Dogs perspire and absorb through their footpads. Be careful where your dog walks and always avoid any area that appears yellowed from chemical overspray.

is suffering from a skin disorder, you should seek professional assistance as quickly as possible. As with all diseases, the earlier a problem is identified and treated, the more successful can be the cure.

Inherited Skin Problems

Sebaceous adenitis affects Standard Poodles more than any other breed. This term describes a hereditary disorder that causes inflammation to the sebaceous glands and the hair follicles. Young animals that are affected experience flaky skin and hair loss, but do not tend to scratch or appear uncomfortable. The type of sebaceous adenitis that affects the Standard Poodle (and other long-haired breeds) has been classified as Type I. This type progresses quickly, and symptoms are treated topically with corticosteroids, principally through shampoos.

All inherited diseases must be diagnosed and treated by a veterinary specialist. There are active programs being undertaken by many veterinary pharmaceutical manufacturers to solve most, if not all, of the common skin problems of dogs.

Parasite Bites

Many of us are allergic to insect bites. The bites itch, erupt and may even become infected. Dogs have the same reaction to fleas, ticks and/or mites. When an insect lands on you, you have the chance to whisk it away with your hand. Unfortunately, when your dog is bitten by a flea, tick or mite, he can only scratch it away or bite it. By the time the dog has been bitten, the parasite has done some of its damage. It

THE SAME ALLERGIES

Chances are that you and your dog will have the same allergies. Your allergies are readily recognizable

and usually easily treated. Your dog's allergies may be masked.

may also have laid eggs, which will cause further problems in the near future. The itching from parasite bites is probably due to the saliva injected into the site when the parasite sucks the dog's blood.

Auto-Immune Skin Conditions

Auto-immune skin conditions are commonly referred to as being allergic to yourself, while allergies are usually inflammatory reactions to outside stimuli. Auto-immune diseases cause serious damage to the tissues that are involved.

The best known auto-immune disease is lupus, which affects people as well as dogs. The symptoms are variable and may affect the kidneys, bones, blood chemistry and skin. It can be fatal to both dogs and humans, though it is not thought to be transmissible. It is usually successfully treated with cortisone, prednisone or a similar corticosteroid, but extensive use of these drugs can have harmful side effects.

Acral Lick Granuloma

Many large dogs have a very poorly understood syndrome called acral lick granuloma. The manifestation of the problem is the dog's tireless attack at a specific area of the body, almost always the legs or paws. They lick so intensively that they remove the hair and skin, leaving ugly, large wounds. Tiny protuberances, which are outgrowths of new capillaries, bead on the surface of these wounds. Owners who notice

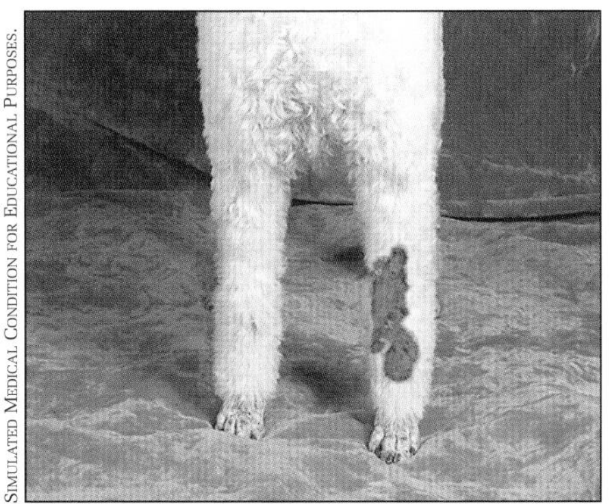

Simulated Medical Condition for Educational Purposes.

An ugly, open wound on the front paw, constantly being licked, is described as an acral lick granuloma. This is a very poorly understood problem in dogs.

their dogs' biting and chewing at their extremities should have the vet determine the cause. If lick granuloma is the cause, although there is no absolute cure, corticosteroids are the most common treatment.

Airborne Allergies

An interesting allergy is pollen allergy. Humans have hay fever, rose fever and other fevers from which they suffer during the pollinating season. Many dogs suffer the same allergies. When the pollen count is high, your dog might suffer, but don't expect him to sneeze and have a runny nose like a human would. Dogs react to pollen allergies the same way they react to fleas—they scratch and bite themselves.

Dogs, like humans, can be tested for allergens. Discuss the testing with your veterinary dermatologist.

This healthy Standard Poodle is not only well exercised and trained but also excited to hear his owner calling him for supper.

FOOD PROBLEMS

Food Allergies

Dogs are allergic to many foods that are best-sellers and highly recommended by breeders and veterinarians. Changing the brand of food that you buy may not eliminate the problem if the element to which the dog is allergic is contained in the new brand.

Recognizing a food allergy is difficult. Humans vomit or have rashes when they eat a food to which they are allergic. Dogs neither vomit nor (usually) develop a rash. They react in the same manner as they do to an airborne or flea allergy: they itch, scratch and bite, thus making the diagnosis extremely difficult. While pollen allergies and parasite bites are usually seasonal, food allergies are year-round problems.

Food Intolerance

Food intolerance is the inability of the dog to completely digest certain foods. For example, puppies that may have done very well on their mother's milk may not do well on cow's milk. The result of this food intolerance may be loose bowels, passing gas and stomach pains. These are the only obvious symptoms of food intolerance, and that makes diagnosis difficult.

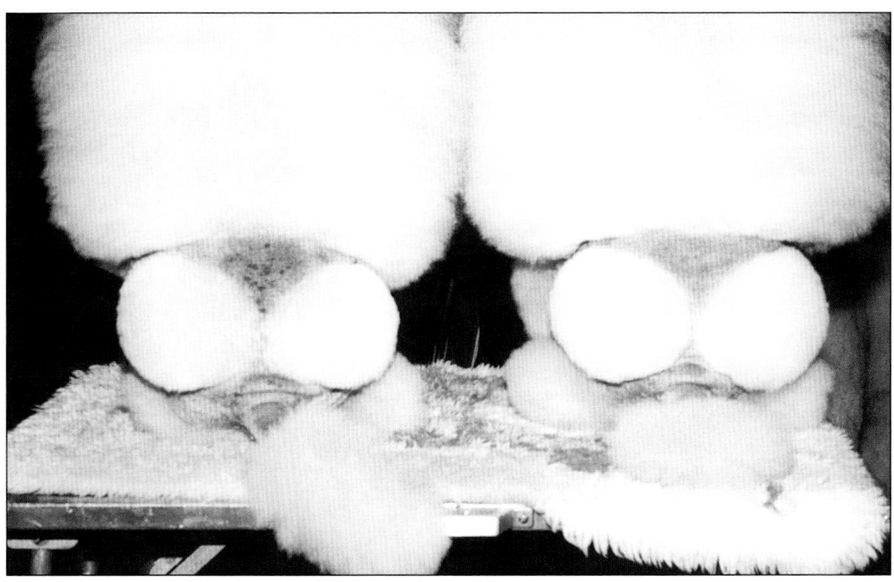

Sometimes, for some unknown reason, a Poodle's skin develops small, round, dark marks. These must be analyzed by your veterinarian to ascertain whether they are melanoma. The dog on the left has the dark spots; the dog on the right is normal.

Treating Food Problems

It is possible to handle food allergies and food intolerance yourself. Put your dog on a diet that he has never had. Obviously, if he has never eaten this new food, he can't yet have been allergic or intolerant of it. Start with a single ingredient that is not in the dog's diet at the present time. Ingredients like chopped beef or chicken are common in dog's diets, so try something more exotic like rabbit, pheasant or another protein source. Keep the dog on this diet (with no additives) for a month. If the symptoms of food allergy or intolerance disappear, chances are that your dog has a food allergy.

Don't think that the single ingredient cured the problem. You still must find a suitable diet and ascertain which ingredient in the old diet was objectionable. This is most easily done by adding ingredients to the new diet one at a time. Let the dog stay on the modified diet for a month before you add another ingredient. Eventually, you will determine the ingredient that caused the adverse reaction.

An alternative method is to carefully study the ingredients in the diet to which your dog is allergic or intolerant. Identify the main ingredient in this diet and eliminate the main ingredient by buying a different food that does not have that ingredient. Keep experimenting until the symptoms disappear after one month on the new diet.

A male dog flea, *Ctenocephalides canis.*

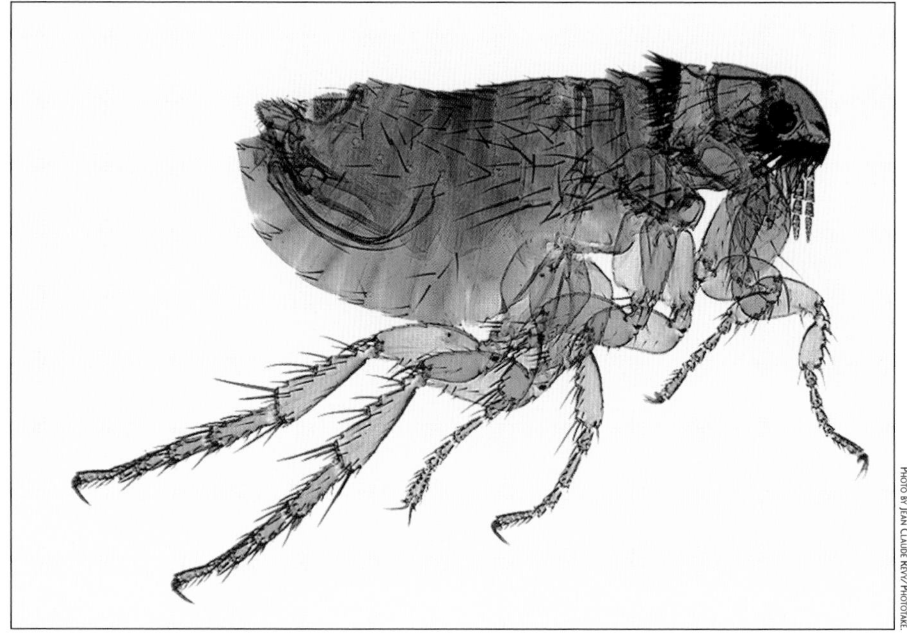

PHOTO BY JEAN CLAUDE REVY/PHOTOTAKE.

EXTERNAL PARASITES

FLEAS

Of all the problems to which dogs are prone, none is more well known and frustrating than fleas. Flea infestation is relatively simple to cure but difficult to prevent. Parasites that are harbored inside the body are a bit more difficult to eradicate but they are easier to control.

To control flea infestation, you have to understand the flea's life cycle. Fleas are often thought of as a summertime problem, but centrally heated homes have changed the patterns and fleas can be found at any time of the year. The most effective method of flea control is a two-stage approach: one stage to kill the adult fleas, and the other to control the development of pre-adult fleas. Unfortunately, no single active ingredient is effective against all stages of the life cycle.

FLEA KILLER CAUTION!

Flea-killers are poisonous. You should not spray these toxic chemicals on areas of a dog's body that he licks, including his genitals and his face. Flea killers taken internally are a better answer, but check with your vet in case internal therapy is not advised for your dog.

Life Cycle Stages

During its life, a flea will pass through four life stages: egg, larva, pupa or nymph and adult. The adult stage is the most visible and irritating stage of the flea life cycle, and this is why the majority of flea-control products concentrate on this stage. The fact is that adult fleas account for only 1% of the total flea population, and the other 99% exist in pre-adult stages, i.e., eggs, larvae and nymphs. The pre-adult stages are barely visible to the naked eye.

The Life Cycle of the Flea

Eggs are laid on the dog, usually in quantities of about 20 or 30, several times a day. The adult female flea must have a blood meal before each egg-laying session. When first laid, the eggs will cling to the dog's hair, as the eggs are still moist. However, they will quickly dry out and fall from the dog, especially if the dog moves around or scratches. Many eggs will fall off in the dog's favorite area or an area in which he spends a lot of time, such as his bed.

Once the eggs fall from the dog onto the carpet or furniture, they will hatch into larvae. This takes from one to ten days. Larvae are not particularly mobile and will usually travel only a few inches from where they hatch. However, they do have a tendency to move away from bright light and heavy traffic—under furniture and behind doors are common places to find high quantities of flea larvae.

The flea larvae feed on dead organic matter, including adult flea feces, until they are ready to change into adult fleas. Fleas will usually remain as larvae for around seven days. After this period, the larvae will pupate into protective pupae. While inside the pupae, the larvae will undergo metamorphosis and change into

EN GARDE: CATCHING FLEAS OFF GUARD!

Consider the following ways to arm yourself against fleas:

- Add a small amount of pennyroyal or eucalyptus oil to your dog's bath. These natural remedies repel fleas.
- Supplement your dog's food with fresh garlic (minced or grated) and a hearty amount of brewer's yeast, both of which ward off fleas.
- Use a flea comb on your dog daily. Submerge fleas in a cup of bleach to kill them quickly.
- Confine the dog to only a few rooms to limit the spread of fleas in the home.
- Vacuum daily...and get all of the crevices! Dispose of the bag every few days until the problem is under control.
- Wash your dog's bedding daily. Cover cushions where your dog sleeps with towels, and wash the towels often.

Fleas have been measured as being able to jump 300,000 times and can jump over 150 times their length in any direction, including straight up.

adult fleas. This can take as little time as a few days, but the adult fleas can remain inside the pupae waiting to hatch for up to two years. The pupae are signaled to hatch by certain stimuli, such as physical pressure—the pupae's being stepped on, heat from an animal's lying on the pupae or increased carbon-dioxide levels and vibrations—indicating that a suitable host is available.

Once hatched, the adult flea must feed within a few days. Once the adult flea finds a host, it will not leave voluntarily. It only becomes dislodged by grooming or the host animal's scratching. The adult flea will remain on the host for the duration of its life unless forcibly removed.

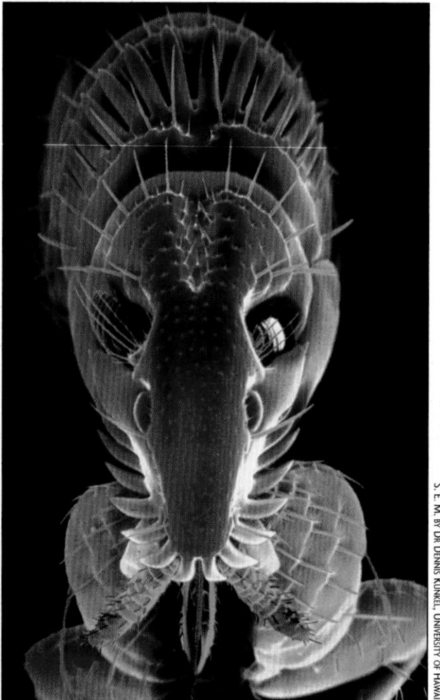

A scanning electron micrograph of a dog or cat flea, *Ctenocephalides*, magnified more than 100x. This image has been colorized for effect.

S. E. M. by Dr Dennis Kunkel, University of Hawaii.

Treating the Environment and the Dog

Treating fleas should be a two-pronged attack. First, the environment needs to be treated; this includes carpets and furniture, especially the dog's bedding and areas underneath furniture. The environment should be treated with a household spray containing an Insect Growth Regulator (IGR) and an insecticide to kill the adult fleas. Most IGRs are effective against eggs and larvae; they actually mimic the fleas' own hormones and stop the eggs and larvae from developing into adult fleas. There are currently no treatments available to attack the pupa stage of the life cycle, so the adult insecticide is used to kill the newly hatched adult fleas before they find a host. Most IGRs are active for many months, while adult insecticides are only active

THE LIFE CYCLE OF THE FLEA

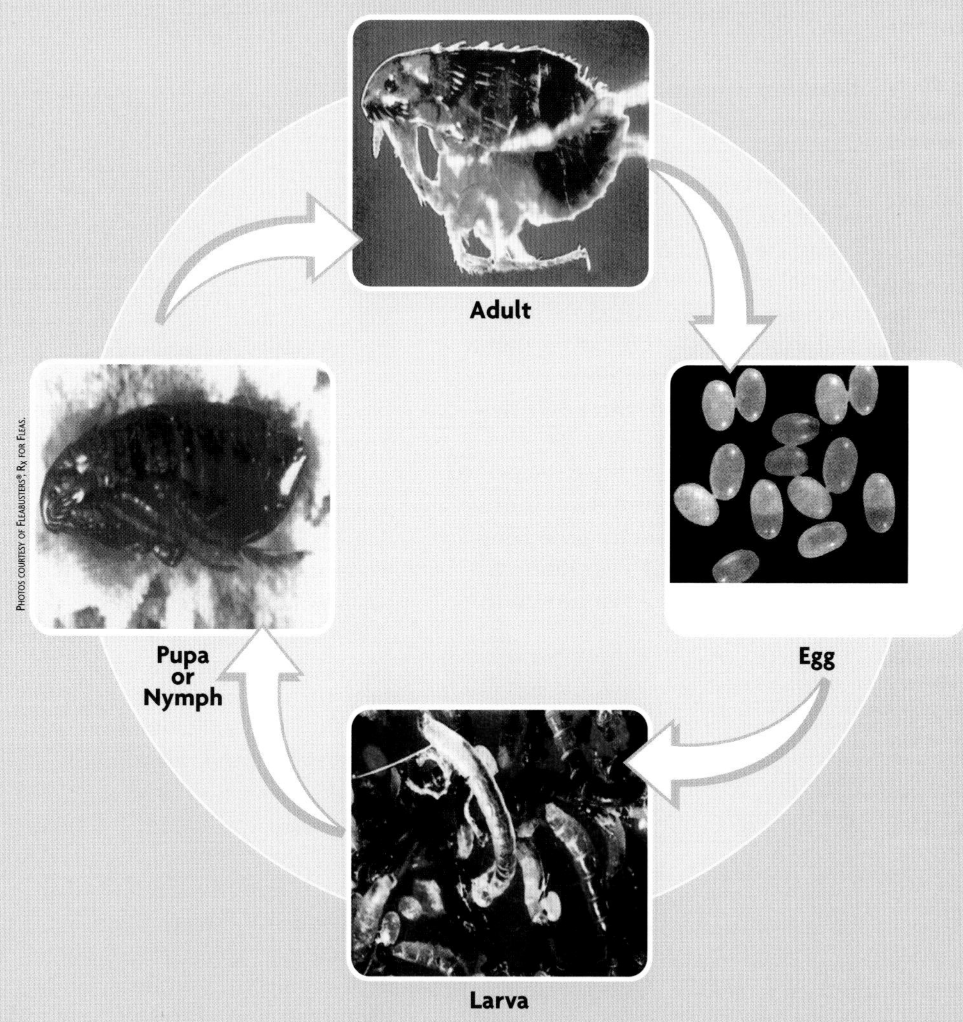

Fleas have been around for millions of years and have adapted to changing host animals. They are able to go through a complete life cycle in less than one month or they can extend their lives to almost two years by remaining as pupae or cocoons. They do not need blood or any other food for up to 20 months.

IGR

Two types of products should be used when treating fleas—a product to treat the pet and a product to treat the home. Adult fleas represent less than 1% of the flea population. The pre-adult fleas (eggs, larvae and pupae) represent more than 99% of the flea population and are found in the environment; it is in the case of pre-adult fleas that products containing an Insect Growth Regulator (IGR) should be used in the home.

IGRs are a new class of compounds used to prevent the development of insects. They do not kill the insect outright, but instead use the insect's biology against it to stop it from completing its growth. Products that contain methoprene are the world's first and leading IGRs. Used to control fleas and other insects, this type of IGR will stop flea larvae from developing and protect the house for up to seven months.

for a few days.

When treating with a household spray, it is a good idea to vacuum before applying the product. This stimulates as many pupae as possible to hatch into adult fleas. The vacuum cleaner should also be treated with an insecticide to prevent the eggs and larvae that have been collected in the vacuum bag from hatching.

The second stage of treatment is to apply an adult insecticide to the dog. Traditionally, this would be in the form of a collar or a spray, but more recent innovations include digestible insecticides that poison the fleas when they ingest the dog's blood. Alternatively, there are drops that, when placed on the back of the dog's neck, spread throughout the hair and skin to kill adult fleas.

Ticks

Though not as common as fleas, ticks are found all over the tropical and temperate world. They don't bite, like fleas; they harpoon. They dig their sharp proboscis (nose) into the dog's skin and drink the blood. Their only food and drink is dog's

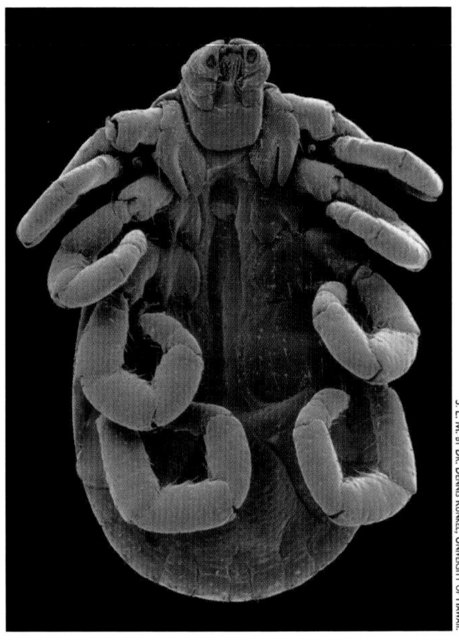

The American dog tick, *Dermacentor variabilis*, is probably the most common tick found on dogs. Look at the strength in its eight legs! No wonder it's hard to detach them.

S.E.M. by Dr. Dennis Kunkel, University of Hawaii.

blood. Dogs can get Lyme disease, Rocky Mountain spotted fever, tick bite paralysis and many other diseases from ticks. They may live where fleas are found and they like to hide in cracks or seams in walls. They are controlled the same way fleas are controlled.

The American dog tick, *Dermacentor variabilis*, may well be the most common dog tick in many geographical areas, especially those areas where the climate is hot and humid. Most dog ticks have life expectancies of a week to six months, depending upon climatic conditions. They can neither jump nor fly, but they can crawl slowly and can range up to 16 feet to reach a sleeping or unsuspecting dog.

Mites

Just as fleas and ticks can be problematic for your dog, mites can also lead to an itchy nuisance. Microscopic in size, mites are related to ticks and generally take up permanent residence on their host animal—in this case, your dog! The term *mange* refers to any infestation caused by one of the mighty mites, of which there are six varieties that concern dog owners.

Demodex mites cause a condition known as demodicosis (sometimes called red mange or

DEER-TICK CROSSING

The great outdoors may be fun for your dog, but it also is a home to dangerous ticks. Deer ticks carry a bacterium known as *Borrelia burgdorferi* and are most active in the autumn and spring. When infections are caught early, penicillin and tetracycline are effective antibiotics, but, if left untreated, the bacteria may cause neurological, kidney and cardiac problems as well as long-term trouble with walking and painful joints.

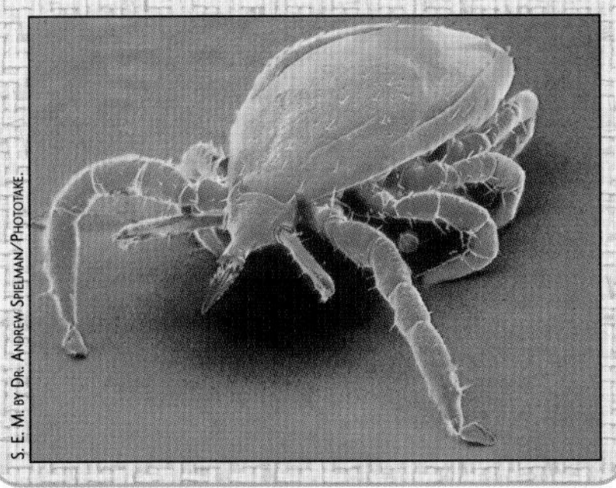

S. E. M. by Dr. Andrew Spielman/Phototake.

Photo by Dr. Dennis Kunkel, University of Hawaii.

The head of an American dog tick, *Dermacentor variabilis*, enlarged and colorized for effect.

The mange mite, *Psoroptes bovis*, can infest cattle and other domestic animals.

Photo by James Hayden/Yoav/Phototake.

Human lice look like dog lice; the two are closely related.

Photo by Dwight R. Kuhn.

follicular mange), in which the mites live in the dog's hair follicles and sebaceous glands in larger-than-normal numbers. This type of mange is commonly passed from the dam to her puppies and usually shows up on the puppies' muzzles, though demodicosis is not transferable from one normal dog to another. Most dogs recover from this type of mange without any treatment, though topical therapies are commonly prescribed by the vet.

The *Cheyletiellosis* mite is the hook-mouthed culprit associated with "walking dandruff," a condition that affects dogs as well as cats and rabbits. This mite lives on the surface of the animal's skin and is readily transferable through direct or indirect contact with an affected animal. The dandruff is present in the form of scaly skin, which may or may not be itchy. If not treated, this mange can affect a whole kennel of dogs and can be spread to humans as well.

The *Sarcoptes* mite causes intense itching on the dog in the form of a condition known as scabies or sarcoptic mange. The cycle of the *Sarcoptes* mite lasts about three weeks, and the mites live in the top layer of the dog's skin (epidermis), preferably in areas with little hair. Scabies is highly contagious and can be passed to humans. Sometimes an allergic reaction to the mite worsens the severe itching associated with sarcoptic mange.

Ear mites, *Otodectes cynotis,* lead to otodectic mange, which most commonly affects the outer ear canal of the dog, though other areas can be affected as well. Dogs with ear-mite infestation commonly scratch at their ears, causing further irritation, and shake their heads. Dark brown droppings in the outer ear confirm the diagnosis. Your vet can prescribe a treatment to flush out the ears and kill any eggs in the ears. A complete month of treatment is necessary to cure the mange.

Two other mites, less common in dogs, include *Dermanyssus gallinae* (the poultry or red mite) and *Eutrombicula alfreddugesi* (the North American mite associated with trombiculidiasis or chigger infestation). The poultry mite frequently lives on chickens, but can transfer to dogs who spend time near farm animals. Chigger infestation affects dogs in the Central US who have exposure to woodlands. The types of mange caused by both of these mites are treatable by vets.

NOT A DROP TO DRINK

Never allow your dog to swim in polluted water or public areas where water quality can be suspect. Even perfectly clear water can harbor parasites, many of which can cause serious to fatal illnesses in canines. Areas inhabited by waterfowl and other wildlife are especially dangerous.

DO NOT MIX

Never mix parasite-control products without first consulting your vet. Some products can become toxic when combined with others and can cause fatal consequences.

INTERNAL PARASITES

Most animals—fishes, birds and mammals, including dogs and humans—have worms and other parasites that live inside their bodies. According to Dr. Herbert R. Axelrod, the fish pathologist, there are two kinds of parasites: dumb and smart. The smart parasites live in peaceful cooperation with their hosts (symbiosis), while the dumb parasites kill their hosts. Most worm infections are relatively easy to control. If they are not controlled, they weaken the host dog to the point that other medical problems occur, but they do not kill the host as dumb parasites would.

A brown dog tick, *Rhipicephalus sanguineus,* is an uncommon but annoying tick found on dogs.
Photo by Carolina Biological Supply/Phototake.

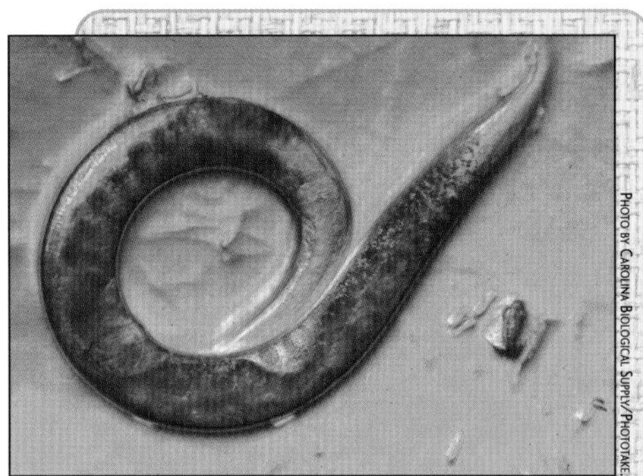

The roundworm *Rhabditis* can infect both dogs and humans.

ROUNDWORMS

Average-size dogs can pass 1,360,000 roundworm eggs every day. For example, if there were only 1 million dogs in the world, the world would be saturated with thousands of tons of dog feces. These feces would contain around 15,000,000,000 roundworm eggs.

Up to 31% of home yards and children's sand boxes in the US contain roundworm eggs.

Flushing dog's feces down the toilet is not a safe practice because the usual sewage treatments do not destroy roundworm eggs.

Infected puppies start shedding roundworm eggs at three weeks of age. They can be infected by their mother's milk.

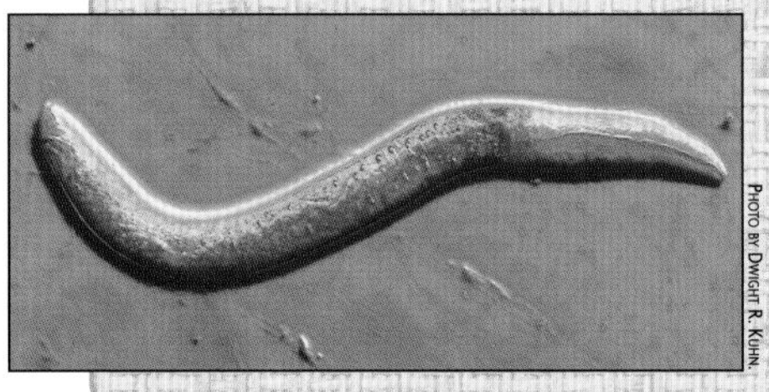

The roundworm, *Ascaris lumbricoides*.

ROUNDWORMS

The roundworms that infect dogs are known scientifically as *Toxocara canis*. They live in the dog's intestines and shed eggs continually. It has been estimated that a dog produces about 6 or more ounces of feces every day. Each ounce of feces averages hundreds of thousands of roundworm eggs. There are no known areas in which dogs roam that do not contain roundworm eggs. The greatest danger of roundworms is that they infect people, too! It is wise to have your dog tested regularly for roundworms.

In young puppies, roundworms cause bloated bellies, diarrhea, coughing and vomiting, and are transmitted from the dam (through blood or milk). Affected puppies will not appear as animated as normal puppies. The worms appear spaghetti-like, measuring as long as 6 inches. Adult dogs can acquire roundworms through coprophagia (eating contaminated feces) or by killing rodents that carry roundworms.

Roundworm infection can kill puppies and cause severe problems in adults, as the hatched larvae travel to the lungs and trachea through the bloodstream. Cleanliness is the best preventative for roundworms. Always pick up after your dog and dispose of feces in appropriate receptacles.

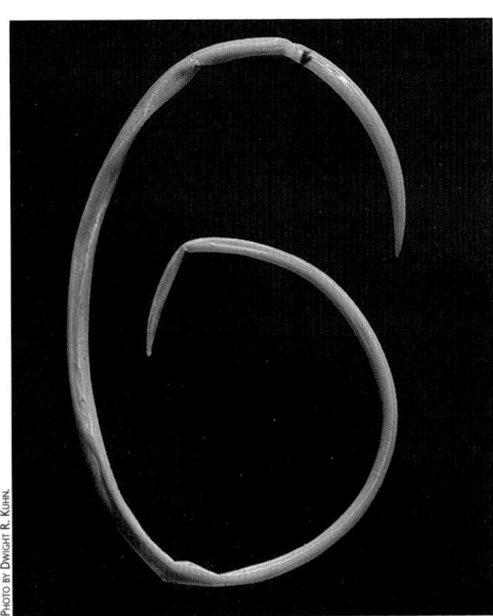

Photo by Dwight R. Kuhn.

The hookworm, Ancylostoma caninum.

Hookworms

In the United States, dog owners have to be concerned about four different species of hookworm, the most common and most serious of which is *Ancylostoma caninum,* which prefers warm climates. The others are *Ancylostoma braziliense, Ancylostoma tubaeforme* and *Uncinaria stenocephala,* the latter of which is a concern to dogs living in the Northern US and Canada, as this species prefers cold climates. Hookworms are dangerous to humans as well as to dogs and cats, and can be the cause of severe anemia due to iron deficiency. The worm uses its teeth to attach itself to the dog's intestines and changes the site of its attachment about six times per day. Each time the worm repositions itself, the dog loses blood and can become anemic. *Ancylostoma caninum* is the most likely of the four species to cause anemia in the dog.

Symptoms of hookworm infection include dark stools, weight loss, general weakness, pale coloration and anemia, as well as possible skin problems. Fortunately, hookworms are easily purged from the affected dog with a number of medications that have proven effective. Discuss these with your vet. Most heartworm preventatives include a hookworm insecticide as well.

Owners also must be aware that hookworms can infect humans, who can acquire the larvae through exposure to contaminated feces. Since the worms cannot complete their life cycle on a human, the worms simply infest the skin and cause irritation. This condition is known as cutaneous larva migrans syndrome. As a preventative, use disposable gloves or a "poop-scoop" to pick up your dog's droppings and prevent your dog (or neighborhood cats) from defecating in children's play areas.

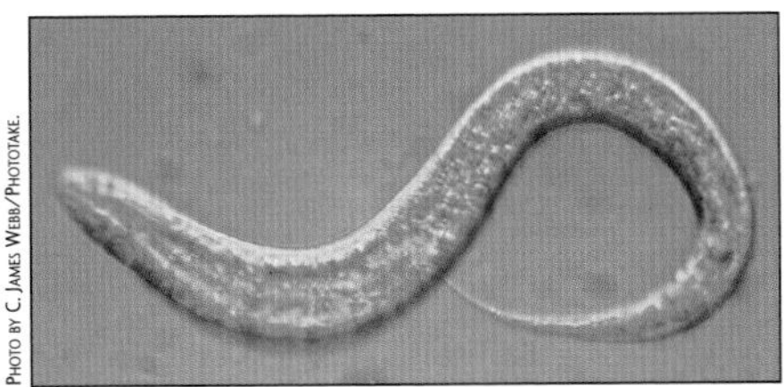

Photo by C. James Webb/Phototake.

The infective stage of the hookworm larva.

TAPEWORMS

Humans, rats, squirrels, foxes, coyotes, wolves and domestic dogs are all susceptible to tapeworm infection. Except in humans, tapeworms are usually not a fatal infection. Infected individuals can harbor 1000 parasitic worms.

Tapeworms, like some other types of worm, are hermaphroditic, meaning male and female in the same worm.

If dogs eat infected rats or mice, or anything else infected with tapeworm, they get the tapeworm disease. One month after attaching to a dog's intestine, the worm starts shedding eggs. These eggs are infective immediately. Infective eggs can live for a few months without a host animal.

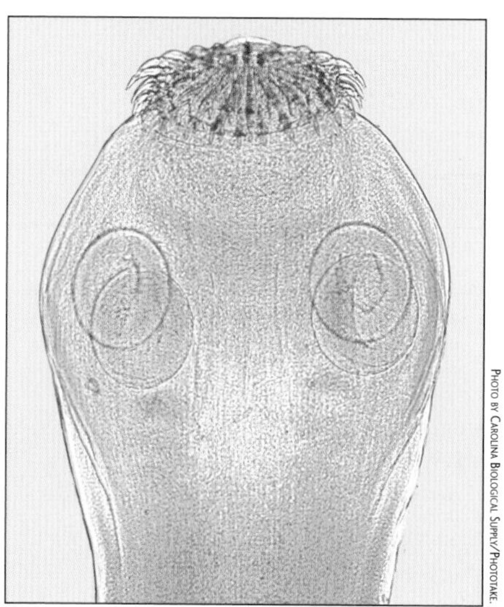

PHOTO BY CAROLINA BIOLOGICAL SUPPLY/PHOTOTAKE.

The head and rostellum (the round prominence on the scolex) of a tapeworm, which infects dogs and humans.

TAPEWORMS

There are many species of tapeworm, all of which are carried by fleas! The most common tapeworm affecting dogs is known as *Dipylidium caninum*. The dog eats the flea and starts the tapeworm cycle. Humans can also be infected with tapeworms—so don't eat fleas! Fleas are so small that your dog could pass them onto your hands, your plate or your food and thus make it possible for you to ingest a flea that is carrying tapeworm eggs.

While tapeworm infection is not life-threatening in dogs (smart parasite!), it can be the cause of a very serious liver disease for humans. About 50% of the humans infected with *Echinococcus multilocularis*, a type of tapeworm that causes alveolar hydatid, perish.

WHIPWORMS

In North America, whipworms are counted among the most common parasitic worms in dogs. The whipworm's scientific name is *Trichuris vulpis*. These worms attach themselves in the lower parts of the intestine, where they feed. Affected dogs may only experience upset tummies, colic and diarrhea. These worms, however, can live for months or years in the dog, beginning their larval stage in the small intestine, spending their adult stage in the large intestine and finally passing infective eggs through the dog's feces. The only way to detect whipworms is through a fecal examination, though this is not always foolproof. Treatment for whipworms is tricky, due to the worms' unusual life-cycle pattern, and very often dogs are reinfected due to exposure to infective eggs on the ground. The whipworm eggs can survive in the environment for as long as five years; thus, cleaning up droppings in your own backyard as well as in public places is absolutely essential for sanitation purposes and the health of your dog and others.

THREADWORMS

Though less common than roundworms, hookworms and those previously mentioned, threadworms concern dog owners in the Southwestern US and Gulf Coast area where the climate is hot and humid. Living in the small intestine of the dog, this worm measures a mere 2 millimeters and is round in shape. Like that of the whipworm, the threadworm's life cycle is very complex and the eggs and larvae are passed through the feces. A deadly disease in humans, *Strongyloides* readily infects people, and the handling of feces is the most common means of transmission. Threadworms are most often seen in young puppies; bloody diarrhea and pneumonia are symptoms. Sick puppies must be isolated and treated immediately; vets recommend a follow-up treatment one month later.

HEARTWORM PREVENTATIVES

There are many heartworm preventatives on the market, many of which are sold at your veterinarian's office. These products can be given daily or monthly, depending on the manufacturer's instructions. All of these preventatives contain chemical insecticides directed at killing heartworms, which leads to some controversy among dog owners. In effect, heartworm preventatives are necessary evils, though you should determine how necessary based on your pet's lifestyle. There is no doubt that heartworm is a dreadful disease that threatens the lives of dogs. However, the likelihood of your dog's being bitten by an infected mosquito is slim in most places, and a mosquito-repellent (or an herbal remedy such as Wormwood or Black Walnut) is much safer for your dog and will not compromise his immune system (the way heartworm preventatives will). Should you decide to use the traditional preventative "medications," you can consider giving the pill every other or third month. Since the toxins in the pill will kill the heartworms at all stages of development, the pill would be effective in killing larvae, nymphs or adults, and it takes four months for the larvae to reach the adult stage. Thus, there is no rationale to poisoning the dog's system on a monthly basis. Lastly, do not give the pill during the winter months, since there are no mosquitoes around to pass on their infection, unless you live in a tropical environment.

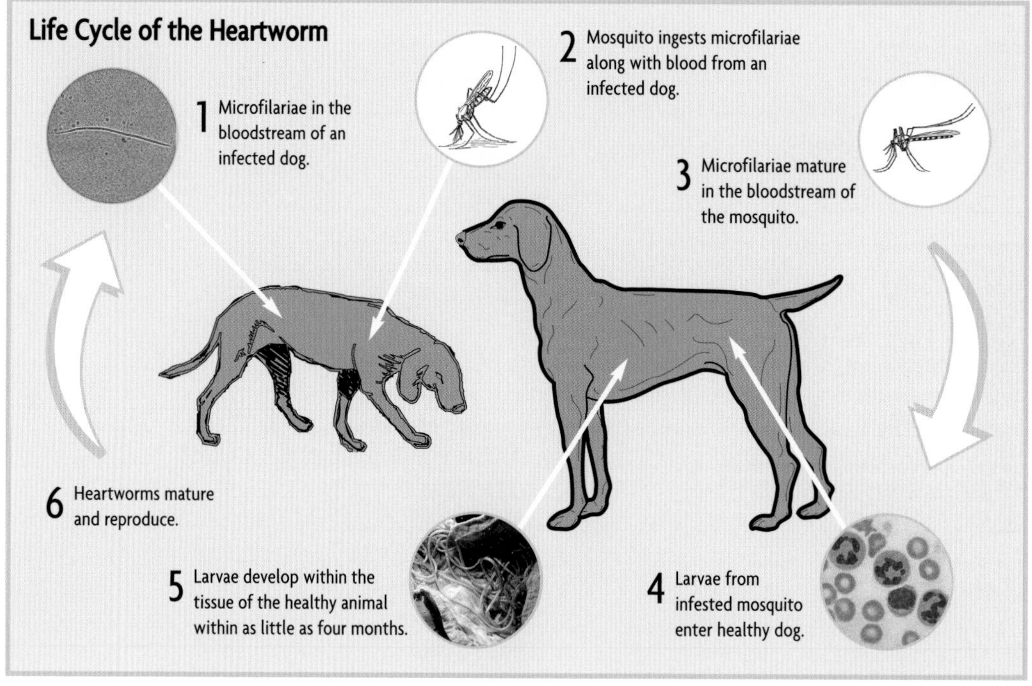

Heartworms

Heartworms are thin, extended worms up to 12 inches long, which live in a dog's heart and the major blood vessels surrounding it. Dogs may have up to 200 worms. Symptoms may be loss of energy, loss of appetite, coughing, the development of a pot belly and anemia.

Heartworms are transmitted by mosquitoes. The mosquito drinks the blood of an infected dog and takes in larvae with the blood. The larvae, called microfilariae, develop within the body of the mosquito and are passed on to the next dog bitten after the larvae mature. It takes two to three weeks for the larvae to develop to the infective stage within the body of the mosquito. Dogs are usually treated at about six weeks of age and maintained on a prophylactic dose given monthly.

Blood testing for heartworms is not necessarily indicative of how seriously your dog is infected. Although this is a dangerous disease, it is not easy for a dog to be infected. Discuss the various preventatives with your vet, as there are many different types now available. Together you can decide on a safe course of prevention for your dog.

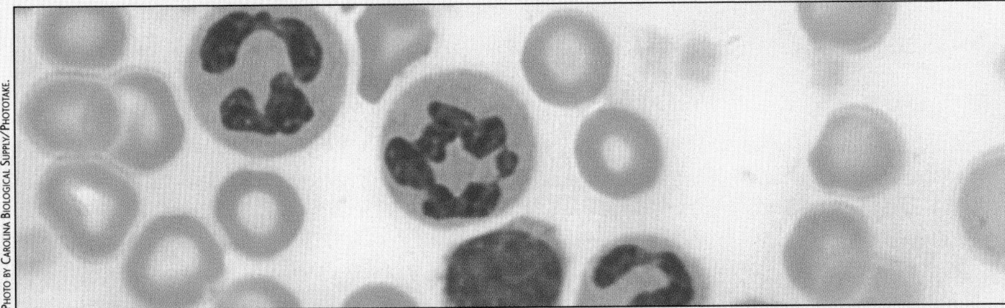

Photo by Carolina Biological Supply/Phototake.

Magnified heartworm larvae, *Dirofilaria immitis.*

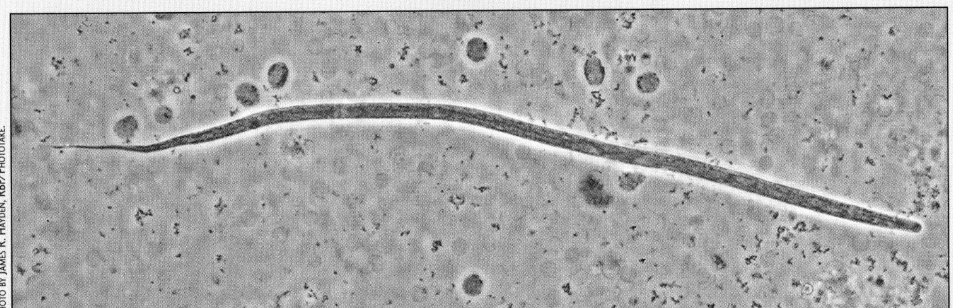

Photo by James R. Hayden, RBP/Phototake.

Heartworm, *Dirofilaria immitis.*

Photo by James R. Hayden, RBP/Phototake.

The heart of a dog infected with canine heartworm, *Dirofilaria immitis.*

YOUR SENIOR POODLE

The term "old" is a qualitative term. For dogs, as well as their masters, old is relative. Certainly we can all distinguish between a puppy Poodle and an adult Poodle—there are the obvious physical traits, such as size, appearance and coat, and personality traits. Puppies and young dogs like to play with children. Children's natural exuberance is a good match for the seemingly endless energy of young dogs. They like to run, jump, chase and retrieve. When dogs grow older and cease their interaction with children, they are often thought of as being too old to play with the kids.

On the other hand, if a Poodle is only exposed to people over 60 years of age, his life will normally be less active and he will not seem to be getting old as his activity level slows down.

If people live to be 100 years old, dogs live to be 20 years old. While this is a good rule of

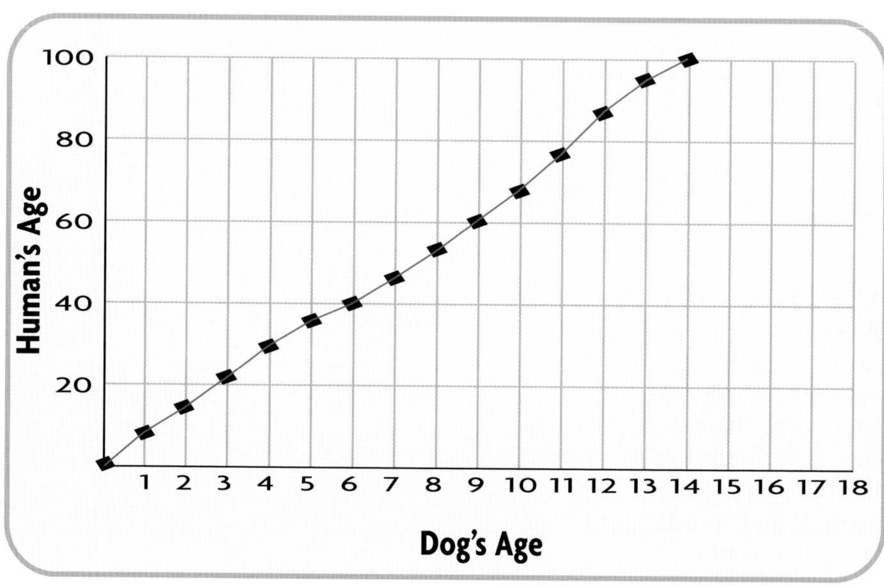

thumb, it is very inaccurate. When trying to compare dog years to human years, you cannot make a generalization about all dogs. Poodles are long-lived dogs, and it can be proposed that smaller Poodles live longer than larger Poodles. Thus, the Toy Poodle can be expected to live 15 years or more; the Miniature, 13 years or more; and the Standard, 10 years or more. It is not uncommon, however, for Toy Poodles to reach nearly 20 years of age. Generally they are hardy and healthy dogs.

Most dogs are considered mature within three years, but they can reproduce even earlier. So, again to generalize, the first three years of a dog's life are like seven times that of comparable humans. That means that a 3-year-old dog is like a 21-year-old human. However, as the curve of comparison shows, there is no hard and fast rule for comparing dog and human ages. The comparison is made even more difficult, for not all humans age at the same rate...and human females live longer than human males.

WHAT TO LOOK FOR IN SENIORS

Most veterinarians and behaviorists use the seven-year mark as the time to consider a dog a "senior." The term "senior" does not imply that the dog is geriatric and has begun to fail in mind and body. Aging is essentially a slowing process. Humans readily admit that they feel a difference in their activity level from age 20 to 30, and then from 30 to 40, etc. By treating the seven-year-old dog as a senior, owners are able to

SENIOR SIGNS

An old dog starts to show one or more of the following symptoms:

- The hair on its face and paws starts to turn gray. The color breakdown usually starts around the eyes and mouth.

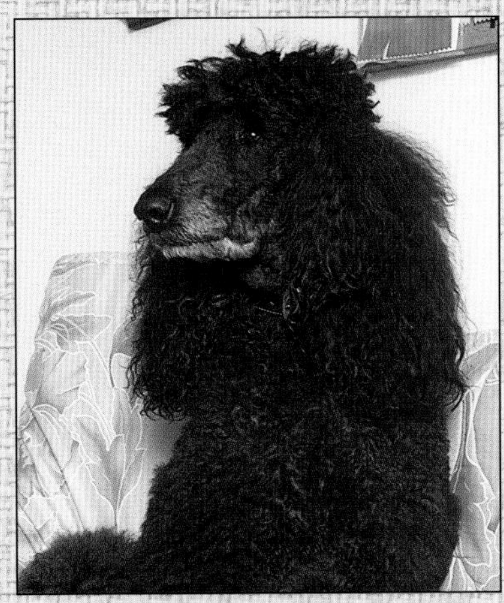

- Sleep patterns are deeper and longer and the old dog is harder to awaken.
- Food intake diminishes.
- Responses to calls, whistles and other signals are ignored more and more.
- Eye contact does not evoke tail wagging (assuming it once did).

NOTICE THE SYMPTOMS

The symptoms listed below are symptoms that gradually appear and become more noticeable. They are not life-threatening; however, the symptoms below are to be taken very seriously and a discussion with your veterinarian is warranted:

- Your dog cries and whimpers when he moves and stops running completely.
- Convulsions start or become more serious and frequent. The usual convulsion (spasm) is when the dog stiffens and starts to tremble, being unable or unwilling to move. The seizure usually lasts for 5 to 30 minutes.
- Your dog drinks more water and urinates more frequently. Wetting and bowel accidents take place indoors without warning.
- Vomiting becomes more and more frequent.

implement certain therapeutic and preventative medical strategies with the help of their veterinarians.

A senior-care program should include at least two veterinary visits per year, screening sessions to determine the dog's health status, as well as nutritional counseling. Veterinarians determine the senior dog's health status through a blood smear for a complete blood count, serum chemistry profile with electrolytes, urinalysis, blood pressure check, electrocardiogram, ocular tonometry (pressure on the eyeball) and dental prophylaxis.

Such an extensive program for senior dogs is well advised before owners start to see the obvious physical signs of aging, such as slower and inhibited movement, graying, increased sleep/nap periods and disinterest in play and other activity. This preventative program promises a longer, healthier life for the aging dog. Among the physical problems common in aging dogs are the loss of sight and hearing, arthritis, kidney and liver failure, diabetes mellitus, heart disease and Cushing's disease (a hormonal disease).

In addition to the physical manifestations discussed, there are some behavioral changes and problems related to aging dogs. Dogs suffering from hearing or vision loss, dental discomfort or arthritis can become aggressive. Likewise, the near-deaf and/or blind dog may be startled more easily and react in an unexpectedly aggressive manner. Seniors suffering from senility can become more impatient and irritable. Housesoiling accidents are associated with loss of mobility, kidney problems and loss of sphincter control as well as plaque accumulation, physiological brain changes and reactions to medications. Older dogs, just like young puppies, suffer from separation anxiety, which can lead to excessive barking, whining, housesoiling and destructive behavior. Seniors may become fearful of everyday sounds, such as vacuum cleaners, heaters, thunder and passing traffic. Some dogs have difficulty sleeping, due to discomfort, the need for frequent potty visits and the like.

Owners should avoid spoiling the older dog with too many fatty treats. Obesity is a common problem in older dogs and subtracts years from their lives. Keep the senior dog as trim as possible since excessive weight puts additional stress on the body's vital organs. Some breeders recommend supplementing the diet with foods high in fiber and lower in calories. Adding fresh vegetables and marrow broth to the senior's diet makes a tasty, low-calorie, low-fat supplement. Vets also offer specialty diets for senior dogs that are worth exploring.

Your dog, as he nears his twilight years, needs his owner's patience and good care more than ever. Never punish an older dog for an accident or abnormal behavior. For all the years of love, protection and companionship that your dog has provided, he deserves special attention and courtesies. The older dog may need to relieve himself at 3 a.m. because he can no longer hold it for eight hours. Older dogs may not be able to remain crated for more than two or three hours. It may be time to give up a sofa or chair to your old friend. Although he may not seem as enthusiastic about your attention and petting, he does appreciate the considerations you offer as he gets older.

Your Poodle does not understand why his world is slowing down. Owners must make the transition into the golden years as pleasant and rewarding as possible.

WHEN THE TIME COMES

You are never fully prepared to make a rational decision about putting your dog to sleep. It is very obvious that you love your Poodle or you would not be reading this book. Putting a loved

A grave marker for a dear, departed Poodle.

dog to sleep is extremely difficult. It is a decision that must be made with your veterinarian. You are usually forced to make the decision when one of the life-threatening symptoms listed above becomes serious enough for you to seek medical (veterinary) help.

If the prognosis of the malady indicates the end is near and your beloved pet will only suffer more and experience no enjoyment for the balance of its life, then euthanasia is the right choice.

What Is Euthanasia?

Euthanasia derives from the Greek, meaning "good death." In other words, it means the planned, painless killing of a dog suffering from a painful, incurable condition, or who is so aged that it cannot walk, see, eat or control its excretory functions.

Euthanasia is usually accomplished by injection with an overdose of an anesthesia or barbiturate. Aside from the prick of the needle, the experience is usually painless.

Making the Decision

The decision to euthanize your dog is never easy. The days during which the dog becomes ill and the end occurs can be unusually stressful for you. If this is your first experience with the death of a loved one, you may need the comfort dictated by your religious beliefs. If you are the head of the family and have children, you should have involved them in the decision of putting your Poodle to sleep. Usually your dog can be maintained on drugs for a few days in order to give you ample time to make a decision. During this time, talking with members of your family or even people who have lived through this same experience can ease the burden of your inevitable decision.

The Final Resting Place

Dogs can have some of the same privileges as humans. They can be buried in their entirety in a pet cemetery, which is generally expensive, or, if they have died at home, can be buried in your yard in a place suitably marked with a stone or newly planted tree or bush. Alternatively, they can be cremated and the ashes returned to you, or some people prefer to leave their dogs at the vet's clinic.

All of these options should be discussed frankly and openly with your veterinarian. Do not be afraid to ask financial questions. Cremations can be individual, but a less expensive option is mass cremation, although of course the ashes can not then be returned. Vets can usually arrange cremation services on your behalf.

Getting Another Dog?

The grief of losing your beloved dog will be as lasting as the grief of losing a human friend or relative. In most cases, if your dog died of old age (if there is such a thing), he had slowed down considerably. Do you want a new Poodle puppy to replace him? Or are you better off finding a more mature Poodle, say two to three years of age, which will usually be house-trained and will have an already developed personality. In this case, you can find out if you like each other after a few hours of being together.

The decision is, of course, your own. Do you want another Poodle, perhaps another variety of Poodle or a different breed altogether so as to avoid comparison with your beloved friend? Most Poodle people remain with the breed because they know (and love) the unique characteristics of the Poodle. Then, too, they often know people who have the breed and perhaps they are lucky enough that one of their friends expects a litter soon. What could be better?

Consult your veterinarian or breeder to help you locate a pet cemetery in your area.

SHOWING YOUR POODLE

In the show ring, the Standard Poodle only has two competitors: the Miniature and the Toy! Poodles are the supreme show dogs, naturally gifted with panache and refinement. These are true showmen! Generations of strutting and leaping through circus acts have yielded masterful performance animals. Of course, not every Poodle whelped by every breeder belongs in the show ring. Most breeders estimate that one out of every ten Poodles born should be considered for the show ring.

When you purchase your Poodle, you will make it clear to the breeder whether you want one just as a loveable companion and pet, or if you hope to be buying a Poodle with show prospects. No reputable breeder will sell you a young puppy and tell you that it is *definitely* of show quality, for so much can go wrong during the early months of a puppy's development. If you plan to show, what you will hopefully have acquired is a puppy with "show potential."

To the novice, exhibiting a Poodle in the show ring may look easy, but it takes a lot of hard work and devotion to do top winning at a show such as the prestigious Westminster Kennel Club dog show, not to mention a little luck too!

The first concept that the canine novice learns when watching a dog show is that each dog first competes against members of its own breed. Once the judge has selected the best member of each breed (Best of Breed), that chosen dog will compete with other dogs in its group. Finally, the dogs chosen first in each group will compete for Best in Show.

The second concept that you must understand is that the dogs are not actually compared against one another. The judge compares each dog against its breed standard, the written description of the ideal specimen that is

AKC GROUPS

For showing purposes, the American Kennel Club divides its recognized breeds into seven groups: Sporting Dogs, Hounds, Working Dogs, Terriers, Toys, Non-Sporting Dogs and Herding Dogs. The Standard and Miniature Poodles compete in the Non-Sporting Group and the Toy Poodle in the Toy Group.

approved by the American Kennel Club (AKC). While some early breed standards were indeed based on specific dogs that were famous or popular, many dedicated enthusiasts say that a perfect specimen, as described in the standard, has never walked into a show ring, has never been bred and, to the woe of dog breeders around the globe, does not exist. Breeders attempt to get as close to this ideal as possible with every litter, but theoretically the "perfect" dog is so elusive that it is impossible. (And if the "perfect" dog were born, breeders and judges would never agree that it was indeed "perfect.")

If you are interested in exploring the world of dog showing, your best bet is to join your local breed club or the national parent club, which is the Poodle Club of America. These clubs often host both regional and national specialties, shows only for Poodles, which can include conformation as well as obedience and agility trials. Even if you have no intention of competing with your Poodle, a specialty is a like a festival for lovers of the breed who congregate to share their favorite topic: Poodles! Clubs also send out newsletters, and some organize training days and seminars in order that people may learn more about their chosen breed. To locate the breed club closest to you, contact the American Kennel Club, which furnishes the rules and regulations for all of these events plus general dog registration and other basic requirements of dog ownership.

The American Kennel Club offers three kinds of conformation

BECOMING A CHAMPION

An official AKC champion of record requires that a dog accumulate 15 points under three different judges, including two "majors" under different

judges. Points are awarded based on the number of dogs entered into competition, varying from breed to breed and place to place. A win of three, four or five points is considered a "major." The AKC annually assigns a schedule of points to adjust the variations that accompany a breed's popularity and the population of a given area.

MEET THE AKC

The American Kennel Club is the main governing body of the dog sport in the US. Founded in 1884, the AKC consists of 500 or more independent dog clubs plus 4,500 affiliate clubs. Additionally, the AKC maintains a registry for pure-bred dogs in the US

and works to preserve the integrity of the sport and its continuation. Over 1,000,000 dogs are registered each year, representing about 150 recognized breeds.

shows: an all-breed show (for all AKC-recognized breeds), a specialty show (for one breed only, usually sponsored by the parent club) and a Group show (for all breeds in the Group).

For a dog to become an AKC champion of record, the dog must accumulate 15 points at the shows from at least three different judges, including two "majors." A "major" is defined as a three-, four- or five-point win, and the number of points per win is determined by the number of dogs entered in the show on that day. Depending on the breed, the number of points that are awarded varies. In a breed as popular as the Poodle, more dogs are needed to rack up the points. At any dog show, only one dog and one bitch of each breed can win points.

Dog showing does not offer "co-ed" classes. Dogs and bitches never compete against each other in the classes. Non-champion dogs are called "class dogs" because they compete in one of five classes. Dogs are entered in a particular class depending on their age and previous show wins. To begin, there is the Puppy Class (for 6- to 9-month-olds and for 9- to 12-month-olds); this class is followed by the Novice Class (for dogs that have not won any first prizes except in the Puppy Class or three first prizes in the Novice Class and have not accumulated any points toward their champion title); the Bred-by-Exhibitor Class (for dogs handled by their breeders or one of the breeder's immediate family); the American-bred Class (for dogs bred in the USA!); and the Open Class (for any dog that is not a champion).

An exhibitor is demonstrating her Standard Poodle's gait to the judge in the show ring.

The judge at the show begins judging the Puppy Class, first dogs and then bitches, and proceeds through the classes. The judge places his winners first through fourth in each class. In the Winners Class, the first-place winners of each class compete with one another to determine Winners Dog and Winners Bitch. The judge also places a Reserve Winners Dog and Reserve Winners Bitch, which could be awarded the points in the case of a disqualification. The Winners Dog and Winners Bitch, the two that are awarded the points for the breed, then compete with any champions of record entered in the show. The judge reviews the Winners Dog, Winners Bitch and all the other champions to select his Best of Breed. The Best of Winners is selected between the Winners Dog and Winners Bitch. Were one of these two to be selected Best of Breed, it would automatically be named Best of Winners as well. Finally the judge selects his Best

SHOW RING ETIQUETTE

Just as with anything else, there is a certain etiquette to the show ring that can only be learned through experience. Showing your dog can be quite intimidating to you as a novice when it seems as if everyone else knows what he is doing. You can familiarize yourself with ring procedure beforehand by taking a class to prepare you and your dog for conformation showing or by talking with an experienced handler. When you are in the ring, listen and pay attention to the judge and follow his/her directions. Remember, even the most skilled handlers had to start somewhere. Keep it up and you too will become a proficient handler before too long!

of Opposite Sex to the Best of Breed winner.

At a Group show or all-breed show, the Best of Breed winners from each breed then compete against one another for Group One through Group Four. The judge compares each Best of Breed to its breed standard, and the dog that most closely lives up to the ideal for its breed is selected as Group One. Finally, all seven group winners (from the Non-Sporting Group, Toy Group, Hound Group, etc.) compete for Best in Show.

To find out about dog shows in your area, you can subscribe to the American Kennel Club's monthly magazine, the *American Kennel Gazette* and the accompanying *Events Calendar*. You can also look in your local newspaper for ads for dog shows in your area or go on the Internet to the AKC's website, www.akc.org.

If your Poodle is six months of age or older and registered with the AKC, you can enter him in a dog show where the breed is offered classes. Provided that your Poodle does not have a disqualifying fault, he can compete. Only unaltered dogs can be entered in a dog show, so if you have spayed or neutered your Poodle, you cannot compete in conformation shows. The reason for this is simple. Dog shows are the main

At one of the world's largest and most prestigious dog shows, Crufts, held in the UK, this Poodle won one of the top prizes in obedience.

forum to prove which representatives in a breed are worthy of being bred. Only dogs that have achieved championships—the AKC "seal of approval" for quality in purebred dogs—should be bred. Altered dogs, however, can participate in other AKC events such as obedience trials and the Canine Good Citizen® program.

Before you actually step into the ring, you would be well advised to sit back and observe the judge's ring procedure. If it is your first time in the ring, do not be over-anxious and run to the front of the line. It is much better to stand back and study how the exhibitor in front of you is performing. The judge asks each handler to "stack" (stand) the dog, hopefully showing the dog off to his best advantage. The judge will observe the dog from a distance and from different angles, and approach the dog to check his teeth, overall structure, alertness and muscle tone, as well as consider how well the dog "conforms" to the standard. Most importantly, the judge will have the exhibitor move the dog around the ring in some pattern that he should specify. Finally, the judge will give the dog one last look before moving on to the next exhibitor.

OBEDIENCE TRIALS

Obedience trials in the US trace back to the early 1930s when organized obedience training was developed to demonstrate how well dog and owner could work together. The pioneer of obedience trials is Mrs. Helen Whitehouse Walker, a Standard Poodle fancier, who designed a series of exercises after the Associated Sheep, Police Army Dog Society of Great Britain. Since the days of Mrs. Walker, obedience trials have grown by leaps and bounds, and today there are over 2,000 trials held in the US every year, with more than 100,000 dogs competing. Any AKC-registered dog can enter an obedience trial, regardless of conformational disqualifications or neutering.

A well-trained Poodle, performing with ease as he climbs up and over the A-frame at an agility trial.

Obedience trials are divided into three levels of progressive difficulty. At the first level, the

Novice, dogs compete for the title Companion Dog (CD); at the intermediate level, the Open, dogs compete for the title Companion Dog Excellent (CDX); and at the advanced level, dogs compete for the title Utility Dog (UD). A perfect score at any level is 200, and a dog must score 170 or better to earn a "leg," of which three are needed to earn the title. To earn points, the dog must score more than 50% of the available points in each exercise; the possible points range from 20 to 40.

Once a dog has earned the UD title, he can compete with other proven obedience dogs for the coveted title of Utility Dog Excellent (UDX), which requires that the dog win "legs" in ten shows. Utility Dogs who earn "legs" in Open B and Utility B earn points toward their Obedience Trial Champion title. In 1977, the title Obedience Trial Champion (OTCh.) was established by the AKC. To become an OTCh., a dog needs to earn 100 points, which requires three first places in Open B and Utility under three different judges.

AGILITY TRIALS

Having had its origins in the UK back in 1977, AKC agility had its official beginning in the US in August 1994, when the first licensed agility trials were held.

Standard Poodle, emerging from a collapsible tunnel obstacle during an agility trial.

The weave pole exercise is smartly executed by this silver Miniature Poodle.

The AKC allows all registered breeds (including Miscellaneous Class breeds) to participate, providing the dog is 12 months of age or older. In an agility trial, the handler directs his dog, by verbal commands and hand signals, over an obstacle course that includes jumps as well as tires, the dog walk, weave poles, tunnels, etc. While working his way through the course, the dog must keep one eye and ear on the handler and the rest of his body on the course.

The first organization to promote agility trials in the US was the United States Dog Agility Association, Inc. (USDAA), which was established in 1986 and spawned numerous member clubs around the country. Both the USDAA and the AKC offer titles to winning dogs.

TRACKING

Any dog is capable of tracking, using his nose to follow a trail. Tracking tests are exciting and competitive ways to test your Poodle's ability to search and rescue. The AKC started tracking tests in 1937, when the first AKC-licensed test took place as part of the Utility level at an obedience trial. Ten years later in 1947, the AKC offered the first title, Tracking Dog (TD). It was not until 1980 that the AKC added the Tracking Dog Excellent title (TDX), which was followed by the Versatile Surface Tracking title (VST) in 1995. The title Champion Tracker (CT) is awarded to a dog who has earned all three titles. Each successive title requires a dog to follow a more difficult track under different conditions.

INDEX

*Page numbers in **boldface** indicate illustrations.*

Dog's Name ______________________________

Date ______________ Photographer ______________________